THE POLITICS OF GENDER REFORM
IN WEST AFRICA

CONTENDING MODERNITIES

Series editors: Ebrahim Moosa, Atalia Omer, and Scott Appleby

As a collaboration between the Contending Modernities initiative and the University of Notre Dame Press, the Contending Modernities series seeks, through publications engaging multiple disciplines, to generate new knowledge and greater understanding of the ways in which religious traditions and secular actors encounter and engage each other in the modern world. Books in this series may include monographs, co-authored volumes, and tightly themed edited collections.

The series will include works that frame such encounters through the lens of "modernity." The range of themes treated in the series might include war, peace, human rights, nationalism, refugees and migrants, development practice, pluralism, religious literacy, political theology, ethics, multi- and intercultural dynamics, sexual politics, gender justice, and postcolonial and decolonial studies.

The Politics of Gender Reform in West Africa

FAMILY, RELIGION, AND THE STATE

Ludovic Lado

University of Notre Dame Press
Notre Dame, Indiana

Published by the University of Notre Dame Press
Notre Dame, Indiana 46556
undpress.nd.edu
All Rights Reserved

Published in the United States of America

Library of Congress Control Number: 2022951792

ISBN: 978-0-268-20506-5 (Hardback)
ISBN: 978-0-268-20507-2 (Paperback)
ISBN: 978-0-268-20508-9 (WebPDF)
ISBN: 978-0-268-20505-8 (Epub)

CONTENTS

FIGURES AND TABLES

FIGURES

TABLES

ACKNOWLEDGMENTS

This work is the result of an exciting intellectual journey during which I benefited from the support of many good people, whom I wish to thank here. My gratitude goes first to the directors of the Contending Modernities project of the University of Notre Dame, R. Scott Appleby, Ebrahim Moosa, and Atalia Omer, who kindly invited me to join this intellectual adventure on a stimulating subject and provided the needed funding. Critical and constructive feedback from Scott Appleby at different stages of the project has been helpfully challenging. Second, I would like to wholeheartedly thank Emmanuel Katongole, coordinator of the African team of the Authority, Community and Identity Working Groups in the Contending Modernities project. The quality of his leadership and friendship created a framework for intellectual stimulation and great teamwork with Elias K. Bongmba (Rice University), Ebenezer Babatunde Obadare (University of Kansas), and Cecelia Lynch (University of California, Irvine), who have all inspired me by the quality of their work. I also want to acknowledge the kind and gracious administrative support of Dania Maria Straughan, the program manager of the Contending Modernities project.

My work with the Contending Modernities project began in 2013 when I was at the Center for Research and Action for Peace (CERAP) in Abidjan, Côte d'Ivoire, where I benefited from fruitful collaboration with Professor Roch Yao Gnabeli of Université Félix Houphouët-Boigny and the members of his social science research laboratory. My gratitude goes also to my colleagues at CERAP, in particular to Dr. Boris Glodé, who served as my research assistant for this project and many others.

The sabbatical year (2017–18) I spent in the African Studies Program at Georgetown University (Washington, DC) helped me to prepare the manuscript with the help of a grant from the Georgetown University Walsh School of Foreign Service. I thank the Jesuit community of Georgetown University for their generous and friendly hospitality. I am grateful to Professor Scott Taylor, then director of the African Studies Program, and his team for the opportunity they gave me to work with them. I especially and wholeheartedly thank Evan Waddill, a student who served as a junior research assistant to me during the sabbatical year at Georgetown University. She has been a great help to me in finalizing this manuscript through her multiple excellent contributions (including bibliographic searches, literature reviews, translation work, proofreading, and editing suggestions), thanks to which she is practically a co-author of some sections of this work.

Lastly, I wish to thank Stephen Little, the acquisitions editor at University of Notre Dame Press who deemed the manuscript worth publishing.

Ludovic Lado
N'Djamena, Chad
November 15, 2022

AFN	Association des Femmes du Niger
AMUPI	Association Malienne pour l'Unité et le Progrès de l'Islam
ATR(s)	African traditional religion(s)
CEDAW	Convention on the Elimination of All Forms of Discrimination against Women
CIRCOFS	Committee for the Reform of the Family Code in Senegal
FCFA	Franc Communauté Financière Africaine (West and Central African currency)
MCM	married Catholic man/men
MCW	married Catholic woman/women
MDG	Millennium Development Goals
MMM	married Muslim man/men
MMW	married Muslim woman/women
MP	member of parliament
NGO	nongovernmental organization
PDCI-RDA	Parti Démocratique de Côte d'Ivoire—Rassemblement Démocratique Africain
RDR	Rassemblement des Républicains
RHDP	Rassemblement des Houphouëtistes pour la Démocratie et la Paix
UN	United Nations
UPDCI	L'Union Pour la Démocratie en Côte d'Ivoire
USD	United States dollar

YSCM   young, single Catholic man/men
YSCW   young, single Catholic woman/women
YSMM   young, single Muslim man/men
YSMW   young, single Muslim woman/women

Introduction

Domesticating Gendered Modernity

As part of a postcolonial generation, I grew up in Cameroon from the early 1970s in an intellectual context dominated by debates about the relationship between tradition and modernity, as well as between individual freedom and the community. When I was in secondary school, we were required to read and discuss a drama entitled *Three Suitors, One Husband* by Cameroonian novelist Guillaume Oyono-Mbia. Women's freedom of choice in marriage is the major theme in this work, which was first published in 1964, barely four years after Cameroon gained its independence from the French and the English.

Juliette, the main character of *Three Suitors, One Husband*, is a secondary school girl who wishes to marry someone of her own choice, a penniless schoolmate. But her parents and grandparents have a different idea of the ideal suitor and of how to choose him. They believe he should be as rich as possible in order to provide for them, and they believe that they should have the last word on whom Juliette should marry. In the process of seeking the highest dowry for their daughter, they become entangled with three suitors.

The first suitor to approach Juliette's parents is a young, hardworking peasant from the village, and they agree with him upon a dowry of 100,000 FCFA (about $200 USD). Afterward, a well-off civil servant shows up who is willing to offer 200,000 FCFA to marry Juliette. Her parents are excited about the prospects such an in-law provides for them, and they decide to reimburse the first suitor. At this stage, they bring Juliette into the picture and inform her of the marriage arrangements being made on her behalf. Her parents and grandparents expect her to marry, as soon as possible, the civil servant whom she had never met. But to their dismay, she opposes the idea. In the face of Juliette's insistence on marrying a suitor of her own choice, her disappointed grandfather declares to her parents: "This is proving me right. I have always told you never to send your girls to school." He compares Juliette to her cousin, who did not attend school and who "always conducts herself as a wise and submissive girl." Then he declares, "Eeeh! The world is spoiled. Schools have spoiled everything! Everything!" (Oyono-Mbia 1964, 30).

Since her parents will only allow her to marry her schoolmate if he is able to offer a larger dowry than the first two suitors, Juliette decides to plot with him to steal from her father the 300,000 FCFA gathered from the first two suitors. The two young people are successful in carrying out their risky plan, and Juliette's parents have no choice but to use the money recovered to reimburse the first two suitors. Juliette ends up marrying the suitor she's chosen for herself without him paying anything. She finds a way to uphold her freedom of choice against the authority of her parents and the larger community.

I grew up from the 1970s onward in an intellectual environment permeated by such attempts of the then-emerging African literature to picture not only the effects of Western culture on African societies but also local responses to these external influences, and especially the gap between older and younger generations. New patterns of living were emerging that were associated with modernity, understood as the influence of the "white man"—so much so that "modern" came to mean "Western" in popular representations of modernity.

When I was asked in 2013 to design a research project as a member of the Authority, Community and Identity Working Groups in the Contending Modernities project at the University of Notre Dame, it did not take me long to settle on exploring gender politics and gender reforms, which I see as a major dimension of African modernity. My choice of this research topic was determined for both contextual and personal reasons. I was based in a research center in Côte d'Ivoire and had just witnessed the controversy sparked by the reform of the Ivorian family code with the aim of enforcing gender equality. Indeed, this controversy was unsurprising, as gender reforms tend to subvert traditional patterns of authority, community, and identity and to enhance the production of new patterns that prize individual freedom and autonomy. Having been born and raised in a patriarchal society in west Cameroon, I did not witness the outright oppression of women by men, but the authority of the husband in the family over his wife and children was taken for granted. The coming of age of gender concerns in Africa is something people of my generation have witnessed as a major and contentious cultural shift of our time.

Securing women's autonomy — their freedom to decide what is best for them — is at the heart of gender reforms around the world. Gender reforms seek to subvert the authority of men over women in social institutions, including within the family and domestic arena. This was certainly the case with the 2013 reform of the family code in Côte d'Ivoire, which I take as a case study in this book. At the heart of this reform was the question of who is (or who should be) the head of the family. Until the reform, the law had stated that the head of the family was the husband. The revised law now holds that it is both husband and wife. Nonetheless, five years after the revision of the family code, the overwhelming majority of men and women surveyed in Catholic and Muslim circles in the city of Abidjan continued to believe that the husband should be the family head (see chapter 3).

By exploring the politics of gender reforms in West Africa, this book seeks to contribute to ongoing debates about the workings of modernity in Africa. The promotion of individual freedom by loosening community control over the individual has been, and still is, a central feature of the making of African modernity. I see current gender reforms that aim to enhance the freedom of women in African societies as one recent component of the implementation of a liberal agenda initiated by the colonial project — an agenda promoting free individuals, free political participation, free markets, free choice, and free sexuality. I argue that in the making of African modernity, African societies struggle to come to terms with the subversion of the authority of local communities and traditional structures through the promotion of individual freedom and the culture of equality that is central to this liberal agenda.

A WORKING CONCEPT OF MODERNITY

Central to my working notion of African modernity is the conflation of modernization with westernization. From this perspective, "modernity" refers to some of the major changes that have occurred in Africa since the colonial encounter. Some of modernity's defining features in the context of sub-Saharan Africa include a modern state and bureaucratization, markets and money, Western science and technology, Western education, the spread of the culture of individualism, the discourse of human rights, and the decline of traditional authorities and institutions.

Concepts of "modernity" and "gender" originated in the West to account primarily for the workings of Western societies at particular moments of their history. Although there is no universal definition of modernity, the term is associated in scholarship with some basic features, such as structural differentiation, secularization, belief in progress, emphasis on personal autonomy, urbanization, primacy of reason, technical specialization, bureaucratization, and pluralization of life-worlds, all of which appeared first in postmedieval European societies (Hefner 1998; Eisenstadt 2000). As S. N. Eisenstadt points out, modernity developed initially in the West and then spread to the rest of the world "above all through military and economic imperialism and colonialism," as well as "through superior economic, military, and communication technologies" (Einsenstadt 2000, 14).

Indeed, modernization in Africa is located within the framework of the encounter between Africa and the West—an encounter deeply rooted in the traumatic violence of the slave trade and colonization. Although in some parts of Africa, through the agency of explorers and missionaries, the "visible aspects of modernization," including "literacy, Western-style education and Western technology" arrived significantly before colonization (Rathbone 2002, 25), colonialism was nonetheless "the historical form through which modernity became a real social project on the African continent" (8). As P. C. Hintzen puts it, "Europe became the prototype of progress to human betterment and the promised future for the colonies." This meant, for the colonized, inclusion in a "new world of development" in which they were considered "almost the same, but not quite" in comparison to "the enlightened modern self." Colonialism itself was legitimized and justified "as the historical route of transition to modernity" (2014, 22).

The intrinsic hegemonic essence of colonialism as a racist economy of violence cannot be discounted (Mbembe 2017, 5). Nonetheless, this book privileges an interactionist approach to the workings of modernity in Africa; that is, I understand modernity in Africa as the outcome of interaction between the modern West and Africa in the framework of colonization. The power structure of this interaction is obviously asymmetrical, because colonization in Africa was essentially a hegemonic program of westernization—of sustained attempts to reshape Africa and its people on the Western model. But that asymmetry does not make Africans passive absorbers of processes like political conquest, monetization, state formation, bureaucratization, and the adoption of new science and technology. Therefore, African modernity, as the outcome of the encounter between Africa and the West, is shaped by both Western and African agencies. In this sense, as Richard Rathbone has argued, "modernization in West Africa has had and will continue to have a distinctly African personality" (2002, 30).

Earlier debates on African modernity have centered on ideas of culture contact and cultural change championed by anthropologists such as Bronislaw Malinowski and Radcliffe Brown (Deutsch 2002, 6). Malinowski described the intellectual and policy challenge of the 1940s, for example, in terms of the cultural engineering of traditional heritage: "The anthropologist has to state, at this point, that human culture is a hard and heavy reality. Man lives in his culture, for his culture, and by his culture. To transform this traditional heritage, to make a branch of humanity jump across centuries of development, is a process in which only a highly skilled and scientifically founded achievement of cultural engineering can reach positive results" (1943, 650).

The project Malinowski describes is still being carried out today. Since the beginning of the colonial period, Africa has been the laboratory for scores of economic, political, and cultural experiments couched as development programs, a major tool of modernization. There is an abundant literature on how modernization theories, developed in the research institutes of Western universities from the 1960s onward by high-flying scholars, were translated into policies to be experimented with in Africa. Most of these hegemonic policies have been largely unsuccessful at generating nonproblematic solutions to the continent's problems (Hintzen 2014; Nabudere 1997; Sklar 1995). Larry Grubbs (2009), for example, who speaks of the "Gospel of Modernization," describes how US-Africa foreign policy was predominantly interventionist and hegemonic during the Cold War. Leading US scholars and policy makers such as Walt Rostow, Elliot Berg, Arnold Rivkin, and Mennen Williams designed theories and policies that demanded Africa's path to development mirror that of the United States and Western Europe. Western Europe, the United States, and major international institutions such as the World Bank and the International Monetary Fund became involved in the effort to effectively claim Africa for Western capitalism in the Cold War context. It is indeed not possible to isolate African modernization from the Cold War, during which Africa became a laboratory for ideological experiments carried out by both communists and capitalists.

Foreign aid was an explicit incentive for African states to follow the policy prescriptions of the United States or the Soviet Union or risk being marginalized. Most Western policy makers claimed to know what was best for the African continent and its people, and these policy makers were not interested in input from African leaders. In Ghana, where Kwame Nkrumah advocated for African unity, the consolidation of resources, and the independent pursuit of economic development, Grubbs writes, "one of the key arguments [Arnold] Rivkin hammered home was the need for African leaders to ignore the siren call of Pan-Africanism" (2009, 68).

Jan-Georg Deutsch (2002) has distinguished two major phases in the modernity debate relative to Africa. The first is that of modernity understood as a historical necessity and marked by the belief that as Africa becomes more rational under the influence of the West, it would of necessity evolve (or progress) from tradition to modernity and become a perfect copy of the West. These 1950s hopes began to fade from the 1970s onward when the paths taken by African countries defied modernization theories, forcing scholars, in the second phase, to adjust their theories in order to acknowledge modernity as a contingent process, especially in the context of globalization (Eisenstadt 2000). Deutsch notes the consequences for conceptions of African modernity of "seeing the contemporary world as characterized by multidirectional global flows of people, ideas and goods and as non- or at best multi-centered": "The potential of this approach lies in the possibility of thinking modernity beyond the idea of linear modernization, wherever its starting point may be located, and beyond European expansion" (2002, 11).

Hegemonic development experiments reached their peak in the 1980s with the imposition of structural adjustment programs in Africa, which, Rok Ajulu points out, are generally accounted as having failed to foster economic growth. Instead, the involvement of the International Monetary Fund and the World Bank in Africa has resulted in "economic stagnation, widespread poverty, and the disintegration of Africa's social fabric on an unmitigated scale." In many countries, even the 1990s wave of democratization seems to "have been captured in the guise of competitive multiparty elections by . . . authoritarian groups" (Ajulu 2001, 29–30; see also Ferguson 2006).

The recent introduction of concepts such as "alternative modernities" and "multiple modernities" signal a critical departure from the homogenizing and hegemonic assumptions of earlier modernization theories. Eisenstadt explains: "While the common starting point was once the cultural program of modernity as it developed in the West, more recent developments have seen a multiplicity of cultural and social formations going far beyond the very homogenizing aspects of the original version. All these developments do indeed attest to the continual development of multiple modernities, or of multiple interpretations of modernity—and, above all, to attempts at 'de-westernization,' depriving the West of its monopoly on modernity" (2000, 25). The distinctiveness of non-Western modernities is based in the selective appropriation of Western modernity in non-Western societies, shaped by particular cultural traditions and historical trajectories. These modernities might draw on varied cultural resources to address problems of the environment, gender, and "new political and international contestations" (25).

Is this true of Africa? Are Africans drawing from their cultural and civilizational traditions to face the problems of modernization? Are environmental and gender policies in Africa freed from the hegemonic entrapments of modernization as westernization? The data I analyze in the chapters that follow suggest that they are not. Gender reforms in Africa still seem to be located within the framework of hegemonic modernities because these reforms are interventionist, elitist, and undemocratic.

A DIFFERENTIATED APPROACH TO GENDER INEQUALITY

Although it is generally assumed that in patriarchal societies women are ruled by men, a differentiated approach to gender power relationships reveals a much more complex picture of Africa. One of the major contributions of gender studies has been to distinguish gender from sex by describing gender as a historical, social, and cultural construction or production, meaning that the differentiation of the social roles and positions of men and women are not given but defined by society, and particularly by those who hold power. Therefore, identifying or being identified as a man, woman, or any other gender category is no longer understood to be innate, but rather to be a social and cultural act (de Beauvoir 1949; Oakley 1972). "Gender" also refers to the social production of sexual categories that in recent decades have challenged the dominant heterosexual norm to make room for other sexual identities (Benjamin 1966; Butler 1990). As the emergence and visibility of the LGBTQ community is still a hotly debated issue in Africa, however, heterosexuality remains the African norm both institutionally and in collective representations. Still, the concept of gender makes it possible to think about the relations between women and men in terms of power relations. This leads to seeing inequalities and discrimination between women and men in society as arising not from biological factors but from social, political, cultural, and economic ones, which can be corrected by adequate reforms.

From 2012 to 2017, I lived in Abidjan, the economic capital city of Côte d'Ivoire, where I taught in a higher education institution. I had many conversations with my students on matters of major decisions about their futures, during which they often said, "I will confer with my uncles," meaning their mothers' brothers. This reminded me that we were living in an environment whose kinship system was predominantly matriarchal. Studies have dwelled on the important role of female rulers in the history of precolonial Africa (Kaplan 1997). The Akan ethnic group, for example, which with 6.5 million members accounts for about 30 percent of the population of Côte d'Ivoire (National Institute of Statistics 2014), is organized into kingdoms (Perrot 2005). In Akan culture, the queen mother has an important traditional role; unlike in many other kingship systems, she is neither the wife nor the mother of the king. Although subordinate to the king, she exerts considerable power in the royal structure. In the absence of the chief, she has full powers, and at the death of the king, it is she who rules until a new chief is chosen. Even more interesting in terms of political power, the Baoule, a major Akan subgroup found in Côte d'Ivoire, venerate as their founding ancestress a female figure called Queen Abla Pokou, whom they claim led them from present Ghana to their current location. She then became their first ruler and was succeeded by another woman, Queen Akoua Bony, who ruled from 1730 to 1760 before men took over the kingdom. Overall, the kingdom has lasted three centuries and has been ruled by twelve sovereigns, three of them women. The third woman, Monique N'ga Tanou, was consecrated by traditional authority on August 31, 2017, under the name Nanan Akoua Boni II. The point here is that patriarchy in sub-Saharan Africa does not necessarily imply male domination in all arenas of social life. This suggests the value of a differentiated approach to gender inequality, which acknowledges the possibility that in some social arenas, men submit to women. This is definitely true of religious power, held in a number of traditional African societies by women, who operated either as healers or as diviners.

Oyeronke Oyewumi warns that even as the understanding of "gender as a social construction" has become "the cornerstone of much feminist discourse," gender studies in Africa should avoid the trap of epistemological and theoretical mimicry—that is, the uncritical assumption that the Western gender conceptual framework applies indiscriminately to non-Western cultures (2005b). Specifically, Oyewumi has pointed out that "if gender is socially constructed, then gender cannot behave in the same way across time and space" (11). Concepts such as man, woman, husband, wife, family, nuclear family, and homosexual can be misleading when uncritically applied to the kinship realities of non-Western cultures. Studying the traditional custom of woman-woman marriage found in some African cultures, Wairimu Ngaruiya Njambi and William E. O'Brien note that the Western "normative presumption of nuclearity" turns "non-Western family forms" such as woman-woman marriage into "bizarre novelties." Indeed, "Several features of western nuclear family ideology go to the root of its alleged functionality: the notions of monogamy and permanence, compulsory heterosexuality or opposite-sex relationships, and the perceived need for a father figure" (2005, 148). Njambi and O'Brien argue for a redis-covery of the many ways in which women strategized to escape male control even in patriarchal cultures like those of precolonial Africa: "By marrying women, these Gikuyu women are clearly radically disrupt-ing the male domination that operates in their everyday lives" (162).

In the same vein, in his introduction to a special issue of the journal *Politique Africaine* on homosexuality in Africa, Christophe Broqua cautioned against simply collapsing the difference between the "social inversion" among the Azande described by E. E. Evans-Pritchard and the meaning of the term "homosexuality" today, given that homosexu-ality is a "historically situated social category" (2012, 23). Others have shown that the priorities of African feminists are quite different from those of Western feminists; whereas the latter focus on gender equality, the former are much more concerned with survival (Mikell 1997b). The point here—one which I entirely support—is that uncritical concep-tual mimicry can be misleading.

Gender as a relational concept describing sexual differentiation is a fundamental dimension of any social organization. Some scholars argue that in much of pre-Islamic and pre-Christian Africa, gender differen-tiation and hierarchies were less rigid, and women's power was estab-lished in a variety of spheres of social life. According to Ifi Amadiume, for example, the importance of the mother figure in royal families made women prominent in many African patriarchal societies (1997, 102). However, this flexibility eroded over time as new religions and European influence introduced a more patriarchal and polarized gen-dered worldview (146), especially with regard to political and religious functions. People's traditional roles within society and religion were reshaped fundamentally, with lasting impacts on modern Africa.

THE GENDER GAP AND POLICY IN CÔTE D'IVOIRE

Gender reforms and policies in modern societies seek to rectify the problem of women's exclusion and marginalization by addressing the inequalities inherent in the social positions and roles of both men and women. This book focuses on the household sphere, where, in African societies generally, men's authority prevails. This is symbolized by the practice of the dowry, or bride wealth, which is the responsibility of the husband to pay, and which ensures, especially in patrilineal societies, that the wife and children belong to the husband (Koné and Kouame 2005, 85). The 2013 reform of the family code in Côte d'Ivoire challenged exactly this primacy of male authority and privilege in the family, although it is obviously not the only social arena where equality between men and women is lacking. Others include education, politics, and employment.

West African societies are predominantly patriarchal in spite of being structured by both matrilineal and patrilineal systems of kinship (Koné and Kouame 2005). In the collective representations of many societies in sub-Saharan Africa, in ordinary circumstances, women are expected to be submissive to men, who in turn are required to take care of women. In general, women have internalized these expectations. The domestic space is perceived as the female space par excellence; procreation and the nurturing of life are a woman's primary and most noble social roles. In addition, African women are in charge of domestic work, taking care of the house and the family. According to a World Labour Organization study published in 1985, housework or domestic chores alone represent 55 percent of a woman's work time in Africa (Chevalier 2005).

The major implication of this mindset is that girls were raised primarily to be given in marriage and to become good housewives. This partly explains why they lag behind men in Western-style education, formal employment, economic initiative, and political participation. The result is the greater social and economic vulnerability of women in the postcolonial context. In spite of the current crisis of masculinity, many sub-Saharan African women are still overdependent on men, and this has led to all kinds of abuses.

The promotion of gender equity has been on the agenda of the United Nations since the 1970s. Indeed, the last thirty years have been marked by a number of world conferences aimed at sensitizing policy makers to the need to factor gender equity into development policies in order to provide equal opportunities to both men and women. Launched in the 1980s, a Women and Development approach advocated the integration of women in processes of development. Inaugurated with the work of E. Boserup (1983), this approach holds that when women are not incorporated in development, economic progress tends to be achieved at the cost of their marginalization. The valorization of women's contributions is therefore understood to be an important element of economic and social modernization. In the 1990s, the Gender and Development approach flourished and held that improving the situation of women and promoting equality between the sexes necessarily entails questioning unequal power relations that are socially and historically established.

Africa, like many other parts of the world, still has a long way to go to close the gender gap. But overall, as the data of the 2017 Global Gender Gap Report suggests, Africa is progressing, with some nations doing far better than many Western countries. The best performance on the continent is that of Rwanda, which ranks fourth in the world for gender equity. Also doing well are Namibia, South Africa, and Botswana (World Economic Forum 2017).

The 2014 population census of Côte d'Ivoire estimated the total population at about 22.6 million, of which 51 percent live in urban areas and 49 percent in rural areas (National Institute of Statistics 2014). The Ivorian population is 51.7 percent men and 48.3 percent women, but gender gap data suggests that these proportions are not reflected in social structures of political and economic empowerment. According to the 2020 Gender Inequality Index (GII) report of the United Nations Development Programme, Côte d'Ivoire has a GII value of 0.638, ranking it 153 out of 162 countries in 2019 (United Nations Development Programme 2020). Although it is closing the gender gap in areas such education and health, it still has a long way to go on the economic participation of women and their political empowerment.

Since its independence, Côte d'Ivoire has gradually adjusted to the momentum of gender reforms going on at the global level. In this endeavor, the state is but one major stakeholder among many, including nonstate actors such as civil society organizations and the private sector, which rose to prominence following the demise of the welfare state in Africa in the 1990s. The reinforcement of institutional mechanisms for gender promotion, one of the critical aspects of the 1995 Beijing Platform for Action, has become the framework for considering gender in public policies in many countries, and Côte d'Ivoire is no exception. Côte d'Ivoire public policy defines gender equity as "an approach to development which aims at reducing social, economic political and

cultural inequalities between men and women, between boys and girls."
Policy that promotes gender equity "reveals injustices and discrimina-
tions which are encouraged or tolerated in various social contexts, very
often against women," including "chances, opportunities, obligations
and rights awarded to any individual (man or woman)." Appropriate
gender equity policy is that which "comparatively analyzes the situation of men and women, identifies the sources of inequality between
the sexes, and attempts to reduce them." The state also defines gender
as "all the implicit or explicit rules that govern the relationships between man and woman on the basis of different values, responsibilities
and obligations" (Ivorian Government 2009, 10). Notably, this policy-
oriented definition of gender equity does not include concerns about
sexual minorities, such as the LGBTQ community.

Côte d'Ivoire has ratified a number of international conventions
aimed at promoting the rights of women and removing discrimination
and violence against them. In 1995, it ratified the Convention on the
Elimination of All Forms of Discrimination against Women (CEDAW),
which was adopted in 1979—although it did not adjust its national
legislation to conform to the requirements of this convention until
2013. The most recent Ivorian Constitution, written into law on November 8, 2016, reinforces the protection of women's rights in Articles
35, 36, and 37 and calls for the promotion of gender equity in all sectors of Ivorian society.

At the institutional and strategic levels, there has been an Ivorian
ministry in charge of gender issues since 2006, and each successive
ministry has formed a gender committee to ensure that the needs of
both men and women are taken into account in the elaboration, implementation, monitoring, and evaluation of development programs.
The National Assembly now also has a gender committee. But effective operation of this institutional setup remains an issue, despite Côte
d'Ivoire's generation of a Manual for Gender Integration in National
Development Policies and Strategies (2014), a Plan for the Implementation of the National Gender Policy (2014), and a Roadmap for the Implementation of the Convention on the Elimination of All Forms of
Discrimination against Women (2014). Efforts have also been made to
create a comprehensive database on gender issues that includes a database on family, women's, and children's issues; directories of women's
organizations and networks; a gender-based violence database; and a

subregional database on women, gender, peace, and security. Other institutional innovations include the creation of a National Observatory for Equity and Gender by Presidential Decree No. 842 of December 17, 2014, to monitor gender equity in public policies at the national level and to produce and disseminate gender-sensitive data in all sectors of activities. Also, the National Family Council and the National Women's Council were created in March 2014 and March 2015, respectively. To enhance the economic and political participation of women in public life, a Compendium of Female Competencies project was launched in 2011, and this has led to the production of a Directory of Competent Women in various professional fields. Concern about the economic empowerment of women, finally, lies behind the 2012 government's creation of the special Fund for Women in Côte d'Ivoire to facilitate women's access to small credit loans.

The most promising progress, however, has been in the educational sector. This is a major sign of hope, because education has proven to be a significant source of empowerment for women. The General Census of 2014 indicates that the rate of illiteracy in Côte d'Ivoire is 56.1 percent (36.8 percent of men and 63.2 percent of women). The main step the government has taken in response to the problem of illiteracy is to adopt a policy of compulsory schooling, mandated by ministerial decree in 2015.[1] Other efforts include the construction and equipment of school canteens and of separate latrines for girls and boys in schools. Since 2014, young girls who qualify can apply for entry in specialized schools for security forces just as young boys can. At the level of civil society, women's organizations have been instrumental in advancing the cause of women's rights and gender equity in Côte d'Ivoire. Women's rights organizations are becoming more and more numerous; their large numbers do not seem to improve their impact, however, due to a lack of coordination.

Thus, significant efforts have been made in Côte d'Ivoire at the political, institutional, and legal levels to promote gender equity and social inclusion in recent years. Despite these advances, one major concern is how to ensure that reforms do not remain on paper but translate into policies that effectively improve women's conditions. Translating policies into the reality of human development is where African countries most often fail. Institutional reforms alone are not enough.

The push from Western-led international organizations to protect disadvantaged populations has not only promoted the rights of women but also of LGBTQ peoples worldwide. The existence of homosexuality in precolonial Africa is highly disputed, despite recent scholarly evidence confirming its existence (Epprecht 2008; Evans-Pritchard 1970; Gueboguo 2006; Murray and Roscoe 1998; Msibi 2011). Whatever the precolonial status of homosexuality, the fight against HIV/AIDS has been instrumental in giving greater visibility to African homosexuals, who have come to be classified among the highly vulnerable groups requiring special attention (Vangroenweghe 2000; Yao et al. 2012). In most African countries, state homophobia (Currier 2010) coexists with popular homophobia (Awonko 2012; Lado 2011). Post-apartheid South Africa is currently the only country in Africa that has legalized gay marriage and explicitly protected gay rights (Croucher 2002). African states confronted with international pressure to respect sexual minorities have had to take into account local resistance to gay rights. Cultural nationalists suspect the West of trying to use economic conditionality to impose its models of sexuality on Africa (Broqua 2012). They portray any sexual orientation other than heterosexuality as contrary to African cultures and values. The quarrels between African cultural nationalists and homo-nationalists revolve around the accusation of ideological imperialism, which is increasingly leveled against the international mobilization of the LGBTQ community (Broqua 2012; Demange 2012; Currier 2010).

More than half of African countries penalize homosexuality (Itabohary 2012). The Ivorian Penal Code does not explicitly criminalize homosexual acts but, in its second paragraph, Article 360 details sanctions against public indecency involving people of the same sex. LGBTQ Ivorians are targets of different forms of violence (Yao et al. 2012), especially when they strive for more visibility. In French-speaking African countries, most sexual minority organizations were created in 2000 and afterward, thanks to the fight against HIV/AIDS. They have since evolved to also address issues of stigmatization and the abuse of the human rights of members of the LGBTQ community (Broqua 2012). The most prominent such organizations in Côte d'Ivoire include Alternative-Côte d'Ivoire, which chairs the watchdog committee on violence against LGBTQ people at the national level; Arc-en-ciel-plus; Secours Bouaké; and the Lesbian Life Association.

Although in major cities like Abidjan there is a certain degree of tolerance toward the LGBTQ community as long as its members keep evidence of their sexual diversity private (Lepape and Vidal 1984), heterosexuality remains the dominant norm in Côte d'Ivoire. The state tends to turn a blind eye to the existence of LGBTQ organizations, tolerating their visibility for public health reasons related to the fight against HIV/AIDS, in which the LGBTQ community is classified as a component "key population" requiring special treatment (Yao et al. 2012). But state tolerance has its limits, and LGBTQ organizations keep a very low public profile in the homophobic Ivorian social environment. Nor does the state concept of gender in Côte d'Ivoire include the LGBTQ community. As one member of this community put it, "In Côte d'Ivoire, the conception of gender is limited to binary opposition male/female, the equality of man and woman. But they should understand that the concept of gender is broader and evolving. So the national document on gender has a lot of deficiencies in this respect" (Member of the LGBT community, Lesbian Life Association, personal interview, 20 April 2017). Members of the LGBTQ community are not involved in the drafting or adoption of national strategic documents of gender policies, nor do these documents take the existence or needs of LGBTQ people into consideration.

DOMESTICATING MODERNITIES

Hegemony does not necessarily produce homogeneity. Sally Engle Merry speaks of the "vernacularization" and "indigenization" of human rights concepts and ideologies, meaning their adaptation to local contexts and meaning (2006, 39). She distinguishes two forms of vernacularization, with replication at one end and hybridization at the other (44). A process of vernacularization can also fail or be distorted. The shape of hegemonic modernities is as much the result of external intervention as of the responses of local agency (Macamo 2005). Any account of African modernities that does not take African agency seriously is flawed (Rathbone 2002, 19; see also Dlamini 2015). Over time, people have developed their own culturally embedded notions of what they consider to be modern (Deutsch 2002, 4). Writing about grassroots perceptions of modernity in Tanzania, Claire Mercer rightly remarked that "in Tanzania as elsewhere, notions of a future modernity, what it is to be modern and what it means to 'modernize' are constantly under construction" (2006, 245). As these examples suggest, we must understand African modernity as a *domesticated* modernity, shaped and influenced by local culture, history, religious belief, and traditional social mores.

Over the course of my fieldwork for this book in Abidjan, Côte d'Ivoire, I asked interviewees—most of whom were educated urban dwellers fluent in French, and either Christian or Muslim—how they thought of modernity and what images they associated with this category. The responses exhibited an ambivalent attitude toward modernity. The images that emerged from my interviews include those of "change" (*la modernité, c'est le changement*) and "novelty" (*la modernité, c'est quelque chose de nouveau ou pratiques nouvelles*), characterized as both positive and negative and associated with various aspects of social life. One interviewee said: "Modernity is change—the difference between the vision of our forefathers and that of our children today. It is adaptation to current life; it is about new practices" (Ivorian woman in her forties, personal interview, 20 March 2016). The baseline here seems to be the "ways of living of our forefathers," which some refer to as "tradition"; such views can, of course, risk essentializing the ways of the forefathers by denying them the same historicity accorded to modernity. Indeed, as historians have shown, the people of precolonial Africa were as familiar with change as those of any human society.

Some interviewees simply described modernity as "social change" (*changement social*) or as "change of mores" (*changement de moeurs*). But their understanding of change is not confined to ways of being, thinking, or doing. It also extends to material, scientific, and technological innovations, understood as essential components of modernity. Science and technology are perceived as the embodiment of modernity. Interviewees made particular reference to new technologies of communication and information and to new means of transportation, which have accelerated the circulation of people and goods and reconfigured how people inhabit space and time.

Modernity is not only about change, moreover. It was also described by interviewees as people's "ability to adapt" to these changes (*vivre avec son temps*). One is understood to be "modern" if one is open to change and can accommodate novelties. For one informant, "modernity has to do with something new, with things suited for our times [*adapté à notre temps*]" (Ivorian young man, personal interview, February 2016). For another, "modernity is living with one's time, adapting to the evolution of time and space" (Ivorian adult man, personal interview, February 2016). In other words, new times, new ways of living, and new material goods call for adaptation, either by embracing or resisting them. As one interviewee put it, "Modernity is change in present-day society; this change is both positive and negative" (Ivorian adult woman, personal interview, March 2016). For people of faith, moreover, religious norms play a key role in the selective embracing of modernity.

Among the positive aspects of modernity, interviewees mentioned the development of new technologies that have made life easier in many respects. Many spoke of an "improvement of daily living conditions" and of the evolution of "laws governing African realities." Here, change is described in terms of progress: "Modernity is progress—something added onto; that which is new" (Ivorian young man, personal interview, April 2016). Because scientific and technological advances are understood to be the main indicators and drivers of development, modernization since the 1990s has come to be associated with access to information and communication technologies, even though studies have shown that these new technologies have tended to exacerbate social and economic inequalities in Africa, where the majority of people still cannot afford them (Mercer 2006).

In addition to new technology, other celebrated imports of modernity referred to by interviewees include Western schools and the promotion of the rights of vulnerable people, such as women and children. In the words of one informant, "Modernity has allowed women to express themselves as men" (Interview of a male informant conducted in the city of Abidjan in 2016). Modernity is portrayed as a key factor in growing consciousness about human rights, especially those of women, children, and sexual minorities.

But the redefinition of the role of women in society is not welcomed by all. Indeed, modernity is also variously associated by interviewees with a "curse," "debauchery," "social disequilibrium," "depravation of mores," "loss of parental authority," "reconfiguration of family relationships," "neglect of religious norms," "new conceptions of marriage," "the revolt [i.e., the insubordination] of women," "evolution of sexual practices," and "individualism." What stands out in this non-exhaustive list of the charges leveled against modernity is the weakening of parental, male, and family authority in favor of individual freedom or new forms of authority. Some believe the weakening of parental authority is responsible for the demise of good education, since parents are no longer allowed to discipline and guide their children. One man I interviewed expressed his regrets in this way: "Today, children oppose the choices of their parents, and this was not the case in the past. Children claim to have rights: Which rights? It is modernity" (Ivorian Parent 1, personal interview, February 2016). Another added: "You can no longer scold a child, let alone discipline him or her" (Ivorian Parent 2, personal interview, February 2016). In short, diminished parental authority is understood to engender more individual freedom, leading to what some describe as the "uprooting of the youth." This is illustrated, for example, by indecent dressing: "Men and women [no longer] dress in a way that is worthy of religion, and hence the punishment from God," lamented one informant (Ivorian young Muslim, personal interview, March 2016). Modernity is believed not only to weaken traditional forms of family life but also to favor the emergence of new ones, such as gay marriage, described by many as deviant. As one interviewee put it: "Modernity is debauchery with regard to marriage: in the past, a man married a woman; today people of the same sex get [married]. This is not normal" (Ivorian man, personal interview, March 2016). Such comments illustrate the ambivalence of grassroots representations of modernity. It is embraced for its scientific and technological wonders, but it is also associated with moral decline, especially in the family and in sexual ethics.

Elisio Macamo underlines the ambivalence of the "experience of modernity in Africa," arguing that the hegemonic process of westernization in Africa is recaptured and reshaped by Africans to produce new meanings and new subjectivities, which often defy the intended objectives of Westerners. Old and new realities intersect in ways that are not easy to predict or unpack. Under pressure from hegemonic interventionism, Africans have resorted to strategies of adaptation that include both cooperation and various forms of resistance and subversion. Indeed, "constrained by external forces in the choices they make, the practical actions they take and the visions they have," much as they were in the colonial period, Africans "have to define a space and time of their own within the constraints placed on them by these forces" (2005, 11).

Hegemonic modernities in Africa are a laboratory of new subjectivities and meanings that are neither simply imposed nor freely created. Even within the constraints of hegemonic processes, Africans have the capacity to take advantage of the margins of intervention available to them to innovate.

THE SCOPE AND STRUCTURE OF THE BOOK

In her 1969 comprehensive literature review of legal anthropology, Sally Falk Moore remarked, "Anthropologists may not have much of a hand in making the policy decisions . . . but they will doubtless have many opportunities to study a subject they have somewhat neglected: the legislative introduction, and the consequences, of planned change" (1969, 285). The focus of the chapters that follow is not the *what*, or content, of gender reforms but the *how*. The questions that drive the study are captured well by Merry, who asks: "How are transnational ideas such as human rights approaches to violence against women adopted in local social settings? How do they move across the gap between a cosmopolitan awareness of human rights and local sociocultural understandings of gender, family, and justice?" She observes: "Ethnographic research shows that human rights ideas and practices developed in one locality are being adopted or imposed transnationally in a variety of ways. Legal documents and policy statements produced in transnational sites such as UN conferences circulate globally through the work of movement activists and states. Although the historical foundations of human rights and much of their content are Western, they are currently important for social justice movements in many parts of the world" (2006, 38). This study presupposes that the way a legal reform is carried out is as important as the content of the reform itself, and determines the quality of its reception at the grassroots level.

The Contending Modernities project seeks to explore the patterns of interaction between religious and secular forces in the modern world. Gender theories and gender reforms are unquestionably some of the most contentious issues of our modern era, probably because they touch on a fundamental concern of any human society: the regulation of sexuality and marriage. At the center of this regulatory order is control of the reproductive faculties of human bodies, especially women's bodies. The famous French anthropologist Claude Lévi-Strauss argued in his major book on kinship (1969) that the universal phenomenon of the prohibition of incest, which facilitates the exchange of women in marriage, was the first norm that marked the birth of culture; that is, the transition of humanity from nature to culture. Indeed, human societies, and religions in particular, seem obsessed with the regulation of sexuality and marriage. José Casanova wrote that "the politics of gender and gender equality are central to politics everywhere[,] and religion is thoroughly and intimately implicated in the politics of gender" (2017, 57). Regarding Catholicism in particular, he suggested that "The gender question is arguably the most serious and complex challenge facing the Catholic Church today" (57). Of Islam, likewise, Leila Ahmed has explained that because "Family law is the cornerstone of the system of male privilege set up by establishment Islam" (1992, 242), any attempt to reform it is resisted by the leaders who control the religious establishment.

Therefore, this book is not about gender theories in Africa, meaning that it is not directly an argument about the rationality and legitimacy of gender concerns. There is abundant literature on that subject (see Cornwall 2005; Oyewumi 2005a). Rather, this is a study of the politics of gender reforms in West Africa. It focuses on the dynamics of power relationships at play in gender politics and reforms in West Africa in general, and in Côte d'Ivoire in particular. This study seeks to capture the politics of a legislative process entirely driven by the state (see chapter 1) and designed to narrow the gender gap in Ivorian society, and it probes the potential impact of this reform on the condition of women by exploring the practice of civil marriage in Abidjan (chapter 2) and by assessing the reception of the reform among Catholics and Muslims in Côte d'Ivoire (chapter 3). In terms of the Contending Modernities project, I take seriously the role of religions in the public sphere in sub-Saharan Africa. In fact, the chapters that follow show that the outcome of gender reforms in many countries in West Africa depends on the degree of independence of state authorities (the secular) from influential religious organizations. Where state officials depend on religious leaders for popular legitimacy, the latter tend to determine the terms of the reform. This was not case in Côte d'Ivoire, but it is the case in Niger, Senegal, and Mali, which I consider for comparative purposes (chapter 4). The book concludes with an informed reflection on the relationship between religions, the state, and gender reforms that highlights some of the stakes of the domestication of hegemonic modernity in Africa. At the end of the day, the answer to the question "Who is the head of the family?" is negotiated at a crossroads of complex webs of power relationships that structure the international, the national, the local, the religious, and the domestic arenas.

CHAPTER ONE

The Secular State in the 2013 Gender Reform in Côte d'Ivoire

Toward the end of 2012, the government of Côte d'Ivoire tabled a bill in parliament requesting the revision of the family code to enforce gender equality. In less than three weeks, the process in parliament was complete, and the head of state signed the revised legislation into law early in 2013. The single major change to the family code, which sparked a huge controversy, was the removal of the provision that a man is the head of the family and the replacement of a man with a joint and equal leadership of husband and wife. This chapter throws light on the workings of the secular state in Côte d'Ivoire by a reconstruction of the political context and dynamics of the 2012–13 reform of the family code—a process driven by political calculations and lacking in public feedback.[1] I underline the centrality of the power of the modern state as a hegemonic structure in a context wherein religious organizations are not powerful political players. Although the new code was adopted on November 21, 2012, by an overwhelming majority of the Ivorian parliament, these numbers do not actually reflect the convictions of Ivorian MPs on the issue of gender equality. Parliamentarians voted for the new code more to save an alliance born out of the political crisis that plagued Côte d'Ivoire from 2002 to 2011 than from concern for women's rights—which raises important questions about the social legitimacy of the reforms, as well as women's representation in the Ivorian context.[2]

THE POLITICAL CONTEXT OF THE REVISED FAMILY CODE

The ruling political group of Côte d'Ivoire, Rassemblement des Houphouëtistes pour la Démocratie et la Paix (RHDP), was founded in 2005 as a coalition of political parties reclaiming the political ideology of Félix Houphouët-Boigny (1905–93), who ruled Côte d'Ivoire from 1960 until his death. The RHDP was made up of the Parti Démocratique de Côte d'Ivoire—Rassemblement Démocratique Africain (PDCI-RDA) led by Henri Konan Bédié; the Rassemblement des Républicains (RDR) of Alassane Ouattara, the head of state; L'Union Pour la Démocratie en Côte d'Ivoire (UPDCI) of Albert Mabri Toikreuse; Le Mouvement des Forces d'Avenir led by Anaky Kobenan; and L'Union Pour la Côte d'Ivoire of Gnamien Konan. The two major members of the coalition were the RDR of the ruling president and the PDCI-RDA of his close ally, Henri Konan Bédié. These two parties were instrumental in securing the votes necessary to reform the national family code.

The birth of the RHDP coalition was prompted by the long political crisis that destabilized Côte d'Ivoire from 2002 to 2011. The year 2011 witnessed the second round of voting take place in a controversial presidential election in which Alassane Ouattara of the RHDP coalition opposed the outgoing president, Laurent Gbagbo of the Front Populaire Ivoirien. After a long postelectoral dispute marked by violence that caused nearly three thousand deaths, the international community ousted Laurent Gbagbo from power on April 11, 2011, and replaced him with Ouattara, who was sworn in as head of state on May 6, 2011. Thereafter, the country was severely polarized by political cleavages between supporters of Ouattara and the frustrated partisans of Laurent Gbagbo, whom the new regime subsequently sent to the International Criminal Court on November 30, 2011.[3] Legislative elections were organized between December 2011 and February 2012, and they resulted in the overwhelming victory of the RHDP, which then controlled both the executive and parliament. It was in this context that the reform of the family law was initiated.

After the postelectoral crisis, the political parties of the RHDP coalition distributed the political dividends of their alliance by sharing ministerial and other leadership positions at the national level. When the government launched the process of reforming the family code in 2012, it took advantage of its leverage over these appointees to compel its allies to support the project. The 2012 family reform was only made possible in Côte d'Ivoire thanks to political maneuvers within the RHDP.

On November 12, 2012, the draft bill repealing Article 53 and amending Articles 58, 59, 60, and 67 of Law No. 64–375 of October 7, 1964, on marriage, as amended by Law No. 83–800 of August 2, 1983, was presented to the Parliamentarian Committee on General and Institutional Affairs of the National Assembly. In the company of her colleague Anne Désirée Ouloto (the minister of family, women, and children), Matto Cissé Loma (the minister delegate to the prime minister, as well as minister of justice) presented the draft of the new family law after laying out the reasons for the reform. According to these two ministers, while the civil laws enacted in 1964 had in the main contributed to the advent of a modern society, this new law on marriage would help to eliminate all forms of discrimination against women.

The amendment to Article 58 shifted the identification of the head of the Ivorian family from "the husband" to "the spouses." In its original formulation, Article 58 specified that the husband, as family head, fulfills this role "in the joint interest of the household and the children." Article 58 also specified that the "the wife ensures together with the husband the moral and material direction of the family, provides for its maintenance and the education of the children," and only steps in to "replace the husband as family head" in cases where "he cannot express his will." In its revised version, "The family is jointly managed by the spouses in the interest of the household and the children," and both spouses "together ensure the moral and material direction of the family," "provide for the children's education," and "prepare for their future."

Article 59 concerns the financial obligations of spouses. In its original version, "marriage expenses" were "mainly borne by the husband," including the "obligation to provide the wife with everything necessary for her livelihood needs." Failure to do so might result in his being "legally forced to comply." In the revised version adopted in 2013, both spouses are obligated to "contribute to the household expenses in proportion to their respective situations." If either fails in this duty, the other has recourse to the courts "to seize, perceive and keep, in proportion to the needs of the household, part of the salary, work product or income" of the spouse.

Article 60 concerns decision-making regarding where a family lives. In the old version, "The choice of the family residence belongs to the husband, and the wife is bound to live with him, as he is bound to accommodate her." In its revised version, "The family domicile is chosen by common agreement by the spouses," with disagreements to be decided by a judge, "taking into consideration the interest of the family."

Article 67, finally, addresses women's employment. In the original version, the article permits women to work in professions different from their husbands "unless it is established that the exercise of that profession is contrary to the interest of the family." This article was amended in the new family code to give women and men "the right to exercise a profession of their choice, unless it is legally established that the exercise of that profession is contrary to the interest of the family."

THE POLITICAL CONTROVERSY PROMPTED BY THE DRAFT FAMILY CODE

The examination of the draft code by the Parliamentarian Committee on General and Institutional Affairs on November 13, 2012, prompted strong differences of opinion within the RHDP. Most members of parliament belonging to the PDCI-RDA and the UDPCI—both of these parties were part of the RHDP governing coalition—voted against the bill in spite of the fact that it was supported by the chairmen of their parliamentary groups. MPs from the ruling RDR, on the other hand, voted in favor of the draft while condemning the position taken by their PDCI-RDA and UDPCI colleagues. The president of the PDCI-RDA parliamentary group, General Gaston Ouassénan Koné, voiced the reservations of his party and suggested some amendments (Akwaba 2012, 3; see Boga 2012b). He welcomed the initiative as an opportunity for the state of Côte d'Ivoire not only to honor its international commitments but also to reaffirm its commitment to gender equality. He explained, however, that the PDCI-RDA parliamentary group believed that the bill did not take into account the cultural, social, and religious values of Ivorian society, especially in suggesting a model of the family without a single leader. The PDCI-RDA put the following questions to all the parliamentarians:

> Will the absence of a family head not lead to the disintegration of the family unit? Will the absence of the family head not pose a problem with regard to the family's name? Does the absence of a household head not pose a problem with regard to our societal values inscribed in the Bible, the Koran and our traditional religions? Does the absence of a family head bring a real benefit to society, as it is supposed to be the case with any law? (quoted in Akwaba 2012, 4)

In the conclusion to his speech, Koné observed that voting for the proposed law would cause more problems in Ivorian society than it would solve. For all these reasons, the PDCI-RDA ministers in parliament proposed that the principle of a single head of the family be maintained. The chairman of this parliamentary group suggested, however, that the choice of the head of the family should be made by mutual agreement between future spouses before a civil officer during the marriage celebration. This would reflect compliance with the principle of equality between men and women. The UDPCI approved of the amendments suggested by the PDCI-RDA parliamentary group.

While the sixteen MPs from the PDCI-RDA and UDPCI parliamentary groups in the commission voted for the amendments, the seventeen MPs of the RDR voted against them. One MP of the thirty-four present abstained. After the rejection of the amendments, two of the sixteen MPs who had supported them changed their minds when the final vote was taken within the committee. Of the thirty-four MPs present, eighteen voted for the bill, twelve voted against it, and four abstained.

The head of state, Alassane Ouattara, was not happy with this rift within the governing coalition. He interpreted some of his allies' opposition to the draft as a breach of loyalty and decided to dissolve the government coalition in an attempt to send a strong message to the rebelling members of the RHDP that they could lose their government positions as a result of noncooperation. Amadou Gon Coulibaly, the secretary general of the government, observed that opposition from the PDCI-RDA and UDPCI MPs was likely to undermine cohesion within the RHDP, raising a problem of solidarity within the alliance (Depry and Boga 2012, 2). The government was indeed dissolved on November 14, 2012. The prime minister at the time, Jeannot Ahoussou-Kouadio, was reappointed and asked to form a new government. This was an attempt by the executive to put pressure on representatives before the vote in the parliament.

Amadou Soumahoro, both chairman and acting secretary general of the RDR parliamentary group, justified the dissolution of the government with an argument also related to the RHDP alliance. He said it was fitting to obtain the support of all the members of the coalition. He also observed that the dissolution of the government sent a strong message while there was still time for political change, so he called on all members of the alliance to do the right thing—namely, to vote for the new law. He acknowledged that the new law on marriage involved a major social issue on which a political coalition could be divided, but the law as revised would also bring Côte d'Ivoire into compliance with CEDAW, as ratified in 1995. Although members of the ruling coalition were entitled to differences of opinion on this bill, once the debates were over he believed they should support the government: "Either we support the government, in which case we continue to sit in parliament, or we do not support the government, in which case we resign" (Koffi 2012, 3). All the stakeholders were informed that the only condition for the formation of the new government was the final adoption of the revised family code without amendment.

General Ouassenan Koné of the PDCI-RDA, by contrast, reminded the head of state of the obligations of parliamentarians to abide by the constitution and the principle of separation of powers. On November 16, 2012, after meeting with the president of the National Assembly, Guillaume Soro, Koné urged all the parliamentarians to work in serenity. He reminded the public that it was an issue of MPs' freedom of conscience, especially in a republic where the executive, legislative, and judicial powers coexist under the principle of separation of powers (Gbato 2012, 3).

Following this crisis, several meetings between members of the RHDP coalition were held, and as a result the presidents of the rebelling parliamentary groups decided to withdraw their amendments and vote for the law as it was initially drafted (Boga 2012a). On November 21, 2012, parliamentarians voted on the new family law. Of the 229 parliamentarians present, 213 voted for the law, 10 voted against it, and 6 abstained (Ouattara 2012a; Tim 2012). Guillaume Soro addressed the parliamentarians, thanking the presidents of the parliamentary groups for their cooperation. He acknowledged that the bill tabled at the National Assembly deserved to be fully and thoroughly discussed. It was a good law, he said, which he defined as one that crosses centuries while adapting to the evolution of the world, especially as globalization imposes its rules (Ouattara 2012b).

The results of the vote show that the calls of the presidents of the various parliamentary groups to vote for the law were not heeded by all the MPs present—nor did women universally support the measure. In 2012, only 28 of the 229 Ivorian parliamentarians were women. Two of the women actively involved in the reform of the family code were Anne Désirée Ouloto, minister and member of the ruling coalition, and Yasmina Ouégnin, parliamentarian and member of a party belonging to the ruling coalition. Ouloto publicly supported the revision of the law, whereas Ouégnin publicly opposed it. Ouloto, then the minister of solidarity, family, women, and children, said: "With the new law, the woman is no longer a mere helper of the husband in the management of the household. She will no longer have to wait for the husband to be absent or impeded to replace him. The joint management is a source of balance in the family" (quoted in Ouattara 2012a).

Yasmina Ouégnin held a different view. In 2012, she was thirty-three years old and the youngest member of parliament. Ouégnin was born in 1979 in Paris. Her father, Georges Ouégnin, is a well-known political figure in Côte d'Ivoire and was for several decades an ambassador and head of state protocol until the death of former president Félix Houphouët-Boigny. Yasmina Ouégnin, the last born in a family of five, holds a master's degree in business, specializing in insurance and risk management. In addition to her political career, she owns and is the general manager of an insurance company. In 2011, in the aftermath of the political crisis, she was elected member of parliament in the municipality of Cocody in the city of Abidjan, an achievement that many attributed to her father's political influence. She describes herself as an active militant for women's rights and is a founding member of Coalition des Femmes Leaders, an association that promotes women's leadership. She is married and the mother of one child.

Ouégnin's opposition to the revision of the family code, and especially to the provision that a man is the head of the family, attracted attention in the media—particularly because the MP stood her ground against the revision of the code in spite of intense pressure from her party to approve it (Ouattara 2012c, 14).[4] She argued that the function of parliament would be devoid of any meaning if MPs were content to endorse government projects without criticism and without making alternative proposals. In addition, she maintained that countless laws had been passed since independence for the protection of women and children, especially in relation to domestic violence, genital mutilation, the rights to education and health, the work and exploitation of children, the trafficking of children, and the use of child soldiers. All of that legislation had been adopted without any notable effect on society, because none of it had been enforced. It was therefore more important and urgent for the executive branch to rigorously apply the laws already adopted before engaging in futuristic struggles for rights that the population was not demanding.

Ouégnin's second objection to the law pertained to the way it was passed, specifically to the fact that the process of adopting the bill did not respect the separation of powers, a fundamental democratic principle. "It is unacceptable," she argued, "that pressure . . . should be exerted on the legislative to get a law passed" (quoted in Ouattara 2012c, 16). Ouégnin justified her act of defiance of her party in the following terms: "I was of course elected under the banner of a political party, with which I share common aspirations and vision for the development of Ivorian society. But my mandate falls under the legislative power, and it is in that context that my action is inscribed" (16).

While Ouégnin was joined by a handful of dissenters, the vast majority of MPs bowed to the pressure from the executive and the law was adopted.

STAKEHOLDERS WITHOUT A VOICE

There was hardly any public debate about the new family law. While the PDCI-RDA and UDPCI parliamentary groups did raise objections to the content of the law and its potential perverse effects on Ivorian society, the RDR parliamentary group and the executive power focused on the RHDP alliance and the demand for loyalty. The executive was not interested in the debate as much as it was interested in using all means available to get the new family law passed. When the executive branch and MPs who supported the new marriage law did discuss its content, they focused on one major element: Côte d'Ivoire's compliance with CEDAW. The argument in favor of compliance with international law overshadowed all other arguments about the content of the law, its effects, and its impact on Ivorian society. The Ivorian population's understanding of the law and its reception did not seem to be a concern of the executive, which made no move to involve civil society constituencies in the conversation.

Indeed, no stakeholders in the legislation, including religious leaders, leaders of local communities, civil society organizations, citizens, or even legal experts, were given a voice in the debate. Most of the Ivorian population came to know of this draft law only through the press when it became the subject of political controversy. Still, civil society organizations voiced their opinions through the media. The decision of the head of state to dissolve the government during the process of the family code reform was viewed by most civil society organizations as an antidemocratic act. Although Eric-Aimé Semien, president of the NGO Action pour la Protection des Droits Humains, acknowledged that in principle the head of state has the right to dissolve the government, he was concerned about the circumstances of this decision. "Would a simple disagreement between parliamentary groups justify the dissolution of a government when we know that the head of state has other legal means to pass a law?" Semien wondered. "Besides, is it not the essence of the parliament to express all opinions and reservations about laws governing society? Is the parliament not like the agora in ancient Greece?" (2012, 3). For Semien, the MPs' primary concern was to defend the general interest and the deep aspirations of the people, which required them to have freedom and responsibility. He further observed that issues of national and republican interest could not be ignored in favor of pure political calculations, games of alliances, and power struggles that risked emptying the institutions of the republic of their meaning and reducing its leaders to simple stooges.

According to Julien Fernand Gauze, president of the NGO Agir pour la Démocratie, la Justice et la Liberté en Côte d'Ivoire, the dissolution of the government by the head of state was, from a political point of view, an act of sovereignty. Gauze acknowledged that a head of state in a presidential regime like that of Côte d'Ivoire was completely sovereign, but he was concerned about the freedom of the National Assembly in relation to the executive power. He asked, "Does this mean that whenever there are disagreements in the Assembly, we come to the dissolution of the government? Should the two things be intimately linked so brutally and so frontally?" If so, he feared such a move would kill democracy, for debate in the National Assembly would have to be curtailed to avoid government dissolution. If Côte d'Ivoire truly wanted to promote women's rights, on the other hand, he explained that many activities and arenas could be explored: "For example, within political parties, we could gradually move towards parity to allow women to express themselves and enjoy all the rights recognized by the constitution and all international legal instruments applicable in this area" (quoted in Takoue 2012, 3). He believed that the decision to establish shared domestic leadership was too sudden a change and did not take into account all the cultural dimensions of the Ivorian environment.

Less skeptical about the new law, Constance Yaï, former minister and former president of the Ivorian Association for Family Welfare, argued that the law did not in fact make the wife the head of the family, but only recognized the role played by women at home. According to Yaï, the reform was a direct consequence of CEDAW, which had been binding on Côte d'Ivoire since its ratification in 1995. She thought that those who reacted against the new law on marriage simply were not aware that the country had already made that commitment. "When a convention is ratified," Yaï explained, "the logical consequence is to harmonize national laws with that convention" (quoted in Sangare and Lath 2012, 4). She concluded that the law simply put men and women on the same footing, which should not frighten anyone, for it only made women less vulnerable in marriage.

Religious leaders also publicly expressed opinions about the new law. For Imam El Hadj Mamadou Dosso, in charge of documentation and research at the Center for Education and Islamic Research, the revised code belonged "to the category of Ivorian laws which are known to be unsuitable even before their adoption" (quoted in Traoré 2012, 6). The adoption of this type of law, according to Dosso, was made possible by parliamentarians who put their political family and their social promotion above the interests of their people. He believed that when it came to making decisions for the nation, MPs wrongly remained in the headquarters of their political parties instead of consulting their electors. Dosso also questioned the attitudes of civil society organizations and other religious leaders. He believed that if this kind of legislation was adopted, it was precisely because Ivorian civil society was not doing its job of challenging the state to defend the interests of the people. When human rights defenders were promoted to ministerial positions as a reward for their collusion with politicians, they no longer constituted a counter-power to balance public authorities.

With regard to the content of the law, Dosso wondered why the debates focused on the question of who should be the head of the family when other provisions deserved equal attention. Article 67, for example, stipulated that each spouse has the right to practice the profession of his or her choice unless it is judicially established that the exercise of this function is contrary to the interests of the family. Analyzing this article, Dosso wondered: "What will the judge say to the Muslim husband who opposes the sale of alcohol that his non-Muslim wife has chosen as a profession?" Dosso was particularly concerned about the introduction of dual leadership into Ivorian families and believed it would have negative consequences in African society. The smallest social structure is the family, he explained, and the family is organized around sociocultural values. Basing his comments on Koranic verses, Imam Dosso argued that men are superior to women, are responsible for them, and have the duty to take care of them. The suppression of this set of values by the new law amounted to rejecting the will of God and replacing it with the will of men, which flouted both divine principles and the sociocultural values of Ivorian society. Dosso recommended that Africans should live according to their own values, not adopt foreign ones. In conclusion, he requested that measures should be taken to ensure that the scope of the new code, when implemented, did not widen to include other forms of marital life, such as homosexual couples, in the name of freedom and evolution (Sangare and Lath 2012, 4, 7).

Though events showed it was possible to pressure unwilling parliamentarians into adopting a new family law, the question remains whether it has also been possible to impose the acceptance of the law and its application on the population. Some chapters of this book discuss the reception of the law at the grassroots level; for the moment, it is worth asking whether the revised family code has any social legitimacy. The reformed Article 58 stipulates that the family is jointly run by spouses in the interest of the household and children. Both husband and wife have the duty to ensure the moral and material well-being of the family, provide for the education of children, and prepare for their future. One could argue that the removal of the husband-wife hierarchy in family management is difficult to envisage in a stratified or hierarchical society. The joint management of the family implies the actual and compulsory contribution of the wife to the family income. In the old code, which was more in keeping with the way in which traditional Ivorian society operates, the wife had the privilege of being looked after by the husband, who had the obligation to bear responsibility for family expenses. Even if the abolition of the title of head of the family seems to give the woman decision-making power, the lessening of the man's sole financial responsibility for the expenses of the household might be resisted by some women. Ultimately, African cultural norms would make the acceptance and application of the new law on marriage difficult for some women and men. Thus, E. Bela, an Ivorian political analyst, described the disappearance of the notion of the family head as a legal fiction and the concept of an African family without a leader as an illusion. "There is a hierarchy (the husband is the head and the wife the assistant head)," he explained, "which makes family management a joint exercise." By establishing "perfect equality" between man and woman, the new marriage law was "contrary to our African cultures and traditions" and "un-African"—and therefore "inapplicable in our homes" (2012, 4).

By way of illustration, Bela related something he had observed during a wedding ceremony following the adoption of the law:

> In February 2013 in the Brobo Council, a small town near Bouake, when giving the marriage certificate after pronouncing the legal union of the couple, the registrar asked the new family the question about which of the two spouses would receive the certificate. And the woman said that the certificate should be given to her husband. Apparently innocent, that response shows that the idea of a joint management system without a leader is in practice difficult to apply. (2012, 4)

The rapidity of the revised family code's ratification is linked to, and as striking as, the lack of public input prior to its passage. The bill was proposed by the executive and defended in front of the Parliamentarian Committee of General and Institutional Affairs by the minister of justice in the presence of the minister for the family, women, and children. The whole process, including the presentation and examination of the code, parliamentary debates, and consultations within the different political parties, lasted one week. The initial examination of the draft code in the Parliamentarian Committee on General and Institutional Affairs revealed a strong divergence of opinions between the members of the ruling coalition, and it resulted in the head of state dissolving the Ivorian government and reforming the government only after the bill was adopted.

This chapter has demonstrated that the reform of the family code in Côte d'Ivoire was much more a political process than a social and cultural one, as it bypassed significant parliamentary debate and failed to involve nonpolitical stakeholders in the conversation. The top-down approach was predominant, and the voices of civil society were ignored. The major challenge confronting such a process is the social legitimacy of the reform, and ultimately its reception and applicability.

Ultimately, who decides what is best for women in gender reforms? In the Ivorian case, with a parliament overwhelmingly dominated by men, it is obvious that men decided for women, as the latter are underrepresented in political institutions and processes. What does this say about the limits of modern democracies and the devaluing of women's citizenship and their marginalization in political processes and decisions, including those that are ostensibly for their benefit and affect them primarily? In societies that claim to be democratic, women do not have the last word on reforms supposedly meant to improve their condition. This raises the pressing issue of the agency of women in democratic processes within African political arenas often dominated by men.

Moreover, what appears on the surface to have been a national political game was clearly driven at least in part by international dynamics. The reform of the family law provides an example of the domestication of "transnational policy" given that Cote d'Ivoire is a signatory to CEDAW and therefore accountable to a variety of stake-holders. The fact that major stakeholders such as civil society organizations, women's organizations, and religious leaders were ignored by politicians indicates that the main "audience" for the reform was not Ivorian citizens, who had not asked for it, didn't know about it, and, as the next chapters will show, understood the reform as promoting a non-Ivorian "liberal agenda."

CHAPTER TWO

Negotiating Multiplicity

*Authorities, Communities,
and Identities*

To assess the impact of the 2013 reform of the family law on Ivorian society, it is helpful to examine some data on the practice of civil marriage in Côte d'Ivoire. Civil marriage governed by family law is but one type of marriage and empirical evidence shows that, when compared to customary and religious marriage, it is not the most practiced in most West African societies. This fact is particularly important in the assessment of the capacity of the 2013 family law to empower women in domestic spaces.

After a brief historical overview of family law and marriage practices in Côte d'Ivoire since independence, this chapter presents the results of my survey of candidates for civil marriage in Abidjan. These results, which reveal the sociodemographic characteristics of men and women applying for civil marriage in four of the city's municipalities, provide insight into the practice of civil marriage in contemporary Abidjan, as well as some of the effects and limitations of the reform of the family code in a context that asks Ivorians to negotiate multiplicity as they navigate the demands of various authorities, communities, and identities.

FROM THE 1964 FAMILY CODE TO THE 2013 REFORM

Before colonial rule began in 1893, Ivorian law, embodied in the customs and practices of various ethnic groups, was unwritten and fluid. The French colonizers imposed codified statutory law as a superior alternative (Bahi 2014, 151). French principles of justice changed marriage and divorce practices, spousal relations, and inheritance patterns. These changes affected only a minority of Ivorians, however, primarily the still-embryonic urban administrative elite. The rest of the population continued to be essentially governed by customary law. At independence in 1960, Ivorian president Houphouët-Boigny selected the Napoleonic code as the official Ivorian legal body and refused to codify local customs, which the new administration believed to be detrimental to the country's evolution. Instead, Houphouët-Boigny's administration advanced a Western, Christian ideal of the family under a single civil code. The new laws, passed in 1964, regulated family law and reinforced a male-dominated public sphere at the expense of women's rights (Toungara 1994, 47).[1]

The family code enacted by the postcolonial administration in 1964 was culturally challenging in many respects (Abitbol 1966). First, it was a legal consecration of the nuclear family (father, mother, and children) in a context where a considerable portion of the population was of matrilineal descent. In such a context, the Western concept of nuclear family has little relevance because, strictly speaking, children belong to the mother's line of descent. The Akan people, for example, who constitute up to a quarter of the Ivorian population, use two words to describe their kinship system: *abusua*, which means "group of descent," and *fifo* (literally "people of the house"), which means "domestic group" or "residential core." One's *real* family is his or her abusua, not his or her fifo (nuclear family). In the matrilineal kinship system, it is the maternal uncle (the brother of the mother) who has authority over a child, and inheritance is not transmitted from father to son but from uncle to nephew. Although authority in the matrilineal system remains in the hands of men, especially the mother's brother and the father, the mother holds a central symbolic place in the kinship system.

Second, the 1964 family law significantly challenged customary marriage laws by outlawing two major traditional practices—namely, polygamy and the bride price. This change was revolutionary, as Côte d'Ivoire became the first country in French-speaking Africa to adopt such radical measures. In the case of polygamy, the law simply reproduced the formula of Article 147 of the French Civil Code, which stipulates that no one can contract a new marriage before the dissolution of the previous marriage. In polygamous unions contracted before the passage of the new law, the polygamous husband retained the rights acquired through his previous marriages, but he could not contract a new marriage prior to dissolving all the marriages in which he was previously engaged.[2] The prohibition of the paying of the bride price was accompanied by severe penalties, including jail sentences and fines.

Finally, the 1964 law had the effect of granting legal status only to civil marriages by specifying that the state alone could confer legality to marriage. This was an attempt to undercut the importance of traditional and religious marriages. The 1964 act also provided for the principle of freedom of consent. It required men to be twenty years old, and women eighteen, in order to marry. Special dispensations or authorizations could be granted by the president of the republic only for serious reasons, such as pregnancy.[3]

According to A. Touré (1981, 158), the new law was revolutionary only in theory. For it simply endorsed practices already common among members of the Western-educated upper class; it did not seriously impact the lower classes, who had learned to navigate both customary laws and modern laws. Still, the scope of this civil code, which promoted the Western type of nuclear family, and the speed at which it was put into effect were at the root of the many difficulties that arose thereafter.

In addition to suppressing polygamy and the bride wealth and making civil marriage the only recognized type of marriage, the 1964 law on marriage imposed the regime of common property.[4] It specifies that the husband, the head of the family, is responsible for administering the common property of the spouses (Article 74), but the wife replaces the husband as head of the family if he is unable to express his will (Article 58). The wages and incomes of the spouses, as well as all property acquired through purchase during the marriage and any property donated or bequeathed jointly to both spouses, are thus pooled (Article 71). Folquet (1974) argues that the common property regime has the advantage that a woman can legally claim some part of the common property in the event of a divorce. But according to J. Emane, the law unfortunately did not have the desired effect. Emane underlined the lack of freedom of choice between common or separate property, as well as the inequality of the spouses created by the subordination of the woman to man, even in regard to her own property (1967, 87). Some women feared men's use of common income for personal purposes and perpetuated the practice of separate property.

The Association of Ivorian Women (AFI), formed in 1963 as a branch of the ruling party, sought to reinstate certain customary rights by pushing for legislative reform. Though the group was scorned by the media and powerful men who resented these women's efforts, female activists made some political headway, and President Houphouët declared a Women's Year in 1975, creating a women's ministry a year later to advance juridical equality, education, and employment (Emane 1967, 51). The AFI was partially successful due to the membership of women who were wives, sisters, and daughters of the country's political leaders, and therefore could navigate political processes.

In 1983, new civil code amendments recognized the legal maturity and equality of women in the modern nation-state. The law of August 2, 1983, gave spouses a choice between the regime of community of property and the regime of separation of property. In the latter, spouses retain the administration, enjoyment, and free disposal of their individual personal property and own the property acquired individually during marriage. At the dissolution of the marriage, no liquidation or partition takes place, and spouses take back their own personal property. In this system, spouses have only one obligation, that of contributing to the expenses of the marriage to the extent they can.

In recent decades, the struggle for gender equality has become a global issue. International treaties or conventions, once ratified, hold authority over domestic legislation. As we have seen, CEDAW was ratified by Côte d'Ivoire in 1995, but Ivorian domestic law was not harmonized with international conventions on women's rights until 2012. The legally codified notion of the husband as the head of the household placed him in charge of his wife, relegating her to the position of a minor in need of supervision (Bahi 2014, 158). The cornerstone of the 2013 reform of family law was the suppression of the husband's preeminence in the family in favor of gender equality. Indeed, the new Article 58 diminishes the husband's omnipotence and attributes the joint management of the family to the two spouses co-equally. This change has a few legal consequences: it requires women to contribute to the household income and it reinforces the professional autonomy of women. It also requires that the choice of family residence be decided by mutual consent.

Thus, since attaining independence in 1960, the government of Côte d'Ivoire has taken major steps in the direction of reforming the family code to abolish traditional marriage practices, reduce the influence of religion on the solemnization of marriage, and support equality within marriage by giving women greater control over the selection of the family residence, employment, property, and household decision-making. Even after all these reforms, however, as A. G. Kragbe (2019) has explained, in-depth examination of the legislation on the Ivorian family reveals many inconsistencies. There is a real problem, he argues, of the overall harmonization of Ivorian family law with the principle of gender equality introduced in family life by Law No. 2015–33 of January 25, 2013. Some of the inconsistencies pertain to aligning the principle of gender equality with other provisions of the law, such as the notion of paternal power, the choice of family name, and the reciprocal duty of fidelity still marked by discrimination in the penal code. The process of reform is therefore an unfinished business as the new family law is subjected to the test of practice.

In the past, this test has consistently revealed a gap between law and reality. Attachment to traditional practices was a major challenge, as well as a general ignorance of the new laws among all citizens and among women in particular. Widespread illiteracy means that many will never be able to access legal texts directly, so they know neither their rights nor the laws that protect them. Women are discouraged from going to court because of the high cost and intimidating language and proceedings (Bahi 2014, 160). In a case study on women from the Bété and Dioula ethnic groups in Côte d'Ivoire, Risa Ellovich showed that women are less knowledgeable than men about laws. The Bété women, largely Catholic, are more knowledgeable about their rights than the Dioula women, who are Muslim (1985).

A closer look at the gap between the letter of the laws and the realities of Ivorian marriage practices begins to reveal the ways in which the people of Côte d'Ivoire adapt to modernity through the negotiation of multiplicity. Far from accepting the changes to the family code wholesale, they engage in behaviors that reveal their ongoing attachment to customary and religious marriage practices alongside the incorporation of new, state-imposed ceremonies and views. Some Ivorians, mainly a minority of the urban educated and employed, embrace all three marriages and generally in the following order: customary first, then civil, and finally religious. They begin by seeking the blessing of customary authorities by taking their spouse-to-be to visit their parents and securing parental approval. Then, in many cases, the couple will travel to their village (or gather in the family compound in the city) the week before a customary marriage. The following weekend, on Saturday, they are at the mayor's office in the morning for the civil marriage and in church in the afternoon for the Christian wedding. The evening is for the big wedding party, to which friends and relatives are invited.

One of my students was anxious about the reservations of her parents regarding her fiancé. She is Catholic and wanted to know if her parents' reservations could potentially constitute an impediment to her religious wedding. When I told her that from a legal point of view she did not need the authorization of her parents to marry civilly and religiously, she responded, "I cannot marry somebody who does not have the blessing of my parents." State laws regulate only the secular, meaning civil marriage—but clearly, the state ceremony alone does not provide a clear picture of attitudes or practices of marriage in contemporary Côte d'Ivoire.

The key moment in customary marriage, for example, is the payment of the bride wealth by the husband-to-be—a custom prohibited by law but nonetheless widely practiced among Ivorians. My own research and personal experiences suggest that the root of gender equality in Ivorian marriage and family is the institution of the dowry, which, so far, no legal reform has been able to root out. Asked about who should be the head of the family, one of the women I interviewed rhetorically answered, "But who paid my dowry?" In other words, the one who pays the dowry is *ipso facto* the head of the family, and that is the man. Earlier anthropological studies (Radcliffe-Brown and Forde

1950) have shown that the payment of the dowry not only legitimates traditional marriage in most African societies but also is the foundation of the authority of the husband over his wife and his children. This is so much the case that in my own ethnic group, the Bamileke of western Cameroon, a man who takes off with a woman without taking care of customary requirements, especially without paying the dowry, cannot claim ownership of the children he has with her. Both the children and their mother continue to belong to her parents, and the man is not entitled to the dowry of his own daughters until he has paid that of their mother. In a number of cases, the dowry of the first daughter is used to pay that of her mother, at last making the mother's husband a legitimate husband and father.

As these examples suggest, to better assess the impact of the family law reform of 2013, it is important to understand contemporary marriage practices in Côte d'Ivoire. The following section presents some data from a survey of Ivorian couples applying for civil marriage in Abidjan.

THE PRACTICE OF CIVIL MARRIAGE IN ABIDJAN

To apply for marriage under civil law in the city of Abidjan, the future spouses need to file an application comprising a legalized copy of each person's birth certificate, a certificate of residence in the chosen municipality, photocopies of the national identity cards of the spouses-to-be and of their main witnesses, and an application fee of about $100 USD.

According to the 2017 edition of the annual statistics of the Ministry of Interior and Security of Côte d'Ivoire, the demand for marriage under civil law is growing in Côte d'Ivoire (Ministère de l'Intérieur et de la Sécurité de Côte d'Ivoire 2017). As table 2.1. shows, the ten municipalities of the city of Abidjan provided about 60 percent of the total number of marriages registered in Côte d'Ivoire from 2015 to 2017 (over 15,000 marriages per year). In 2006, by contrast, the number of marriages under civil law in the city of Abidjan was 8,885 (Institut National de la Statistique de Côte d'Ivoire 2009). Thus, in a decade, the number has almost doubled.

Table 2.1. Number of marriages under civil law in Côte d'Ivoire

PLACE	2015	2016	2017
Abidjan	15250	15928	15210
Côte d'Ivoire	25689	25678	26316
Percentage	59.36%	62.02%	57.79%

Source: Ministère de l'Intérieur et de la Sécurité de Côte d'Ivoire 2017.

Because of the patriarchal structure of Ivorian society, the decision to get married under civil law remains largely the initiative of men. Many women cohabiting with men patiently, and even anxiously, await the day when their mate will decide to apply for a marriage certificate so that they too can enjoy the prestige of a wedding ring. Marriage under civil law is also beneficial to women insofar as it allows them, in the event of a violation of their rights, to have recourse to tribunals to seek justice—although few women can afford the costs of such judicial procedures. Other advantages include the legal recognition of children, which is required by employers for access to family allowances.

A survey conducted in 1977 by the Ivorian Institute of Public Opinion reported that out of every one hundred women over eighteen living in urban areas, 29 percent were single, 55 percent married customarily, 9 percent married customarily and under civil law, and 7 percent married only under civil law, which makes a total of 16 percent of women married under civil law (Vléï-Yoroba 1997). A few years later, in 1984, twenty years after the introduction of the Ivorian Civil Code, a survey of married men over age fifteen reported that 83 percent had one wife, 14 percent two wives, 2.5 percent three wives, and 0.5 percent four or more wives (Vléï-Yoroba 1997).

Notably, fewer than half of Ivorians marry at all. The 2014 general census results indicate that in the segment of the population aged twelve years and above, only 38.1 percent are married—whether customarily, religiously, or legally. Eleven percent are in a relationship, 47.3 percent are single, and the rest are either widows and widowers or divorcees (National Institute of Statistics 2014). Of the 38.1 percent who are married, 71.9 percent are married customarily, 28.4 percent religiously, and only 8.4 percent civilly (National Institute of Statistics 2014).

This data illustrates the gap between marriage law and the practice of marriage in Côte d'Ivoire. Particularly noticeable is the low percentage of couples married under civil law, the persistence of polygamy, and the resilience of customary marriage (Vléï-Yoroba 1997). A study carried out for this book, in the city of Abidjan in 2017, with the critical help of SDEF-Afrique, confirms this trend. SDEF-Afrique is a local civil society organization whose core activity is the promotion of family law in Côte d'Ivoire. In the various municipalities where SDEF-Afrique is present, a support service has been set up at the civil status office, most commonly in its "marriage section." This type of civil-state partnership tends to improve municipal services and it facilitates access for future spouses to the municipal public service.[5]

Our target population included both couples already married under civil marriage and couples who had formally applied for civil marriage. The main objective of this study was to highlight some of the social and demographic characteristics of couples interested in civil marriage in four municipalities of the city of Abidjan.

The sampling for data collection for this survey began with identification sheets for couples who applied for civil marriage in 2013, 2016, and 2017, after the most recent reform of the family law. These are available at the various town halls of the city of Abidjan. The distribution of the sample within the city of Abidjan appears in table 2.2. Overall, 240 couples were surveyed in four of the twelve municipalities of the district of Abidjan for the three years selected. These figures do not represent the total number of couples who were married or were candidates for marriage in these municipalities during the selected years, but those who agreed to participate in the survey. The choice of these municipalities was driven mainly by pragmatic reasons, as they are the zone of intervention of SDEF-Afrique. SDEF-Afrique's close collaboration with the municipalities facilitated access to the data through the registration sheets of candidates for marriage under civil law, and then to the interviewees themselves.

Table 2.2. Geographic distribution of study participants

Municipality	Number of People			
	2013	*2016*	*2017*	*Total*
Bingerville	20	20	20	60
Koumassi	15	15	15	45
Treichville	15	15	15	45
Plateau	30	30	30	90
Total	80	80	80	240

The description of the couples that follows attempts to identify, first, some sociodemographic and economic characteristics of couples, such as age, religion, ethnic affiliation, and nationality; the level of their academic achievements; the duration of their cohabitation; the marriage type; whether children were born to members of the couple before marriage; the spouses' professional situations; and the family income. Second, the description of the couples attempts to identify spouses' preferences regarding type of matrimony and choice of residence.

Age difference between future spouses. In Côte d'Ivoire, the legal age for civil marriage is twenty-one years old. As shown in figure 2.1, 49 percent of the couples surveyed had an age difference of zero to five years, and 28 percent had an age difference of five to ten years. For these two categories of couples, we can say that marriage occurs between people belonging to the same generation. A total of 20 percent of couples had an age difference greater than ten years, and 1–2 percent exceeded this difference. The oldest male was born in 1944, and the oldest female was born on February 15, 1957. The youngest male was born on December 20, 1997, and the youngest female on April 26, 1997. The biggest age difference between spouses was twenty-nine years; in this marriage, the husband was born in 1963 and the wife in 1992. Given that most spouses selected their partners within their own generation, it can be argued that in contemporary Côte d'Ivoire, arranged or compulsory marriages are on the decline. In the past, parents

Figure 2.1. Age gap between spouses (measured in years)

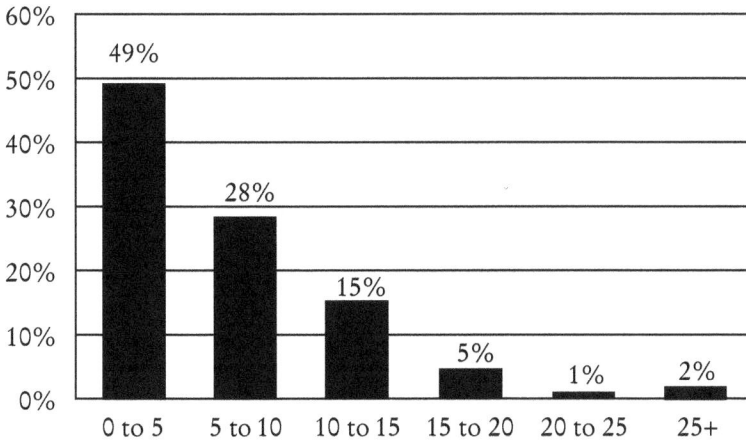

played a more significant role in the choice of the spouses of their children. This has changed considerably in favor of more freedom of choice for future spouses, who often meet and build a relationship before involving their parents in their marriage project (Vimard 1993).

Religion of spouses. Eighty-three percent of couples were members of the same religion, and only 17 percent were not. Of the couples who practiced the same religion, 45 percent were Pentecostal, 32 percent Catholic, 13 percent Muslim, 3 percent Methodist, and the remaining 7 percent were members of smaller religious faith groups, including African Christian independent churches, adepts of traditional religions, and individuals with no religious affiliation. Figure 2.2 gives the gender distribution of interreligious marriage from the sample.

The same proportion (35 percent) of Evangelical and Catholic women married men of a different religion. Of the men surveyed, 33 percent of Catholic men married women of a different religion. Only 13 percent of Evangelical men, however, married women of a different religion. Among Methodists, 23 percent of men and 18 percent of women married outside their religion. For Muslims, 10 percent of women married men of another religion, and 8 percent of men married women of another religion.

Figure 2.2. Gender distribution in interreligious marriages

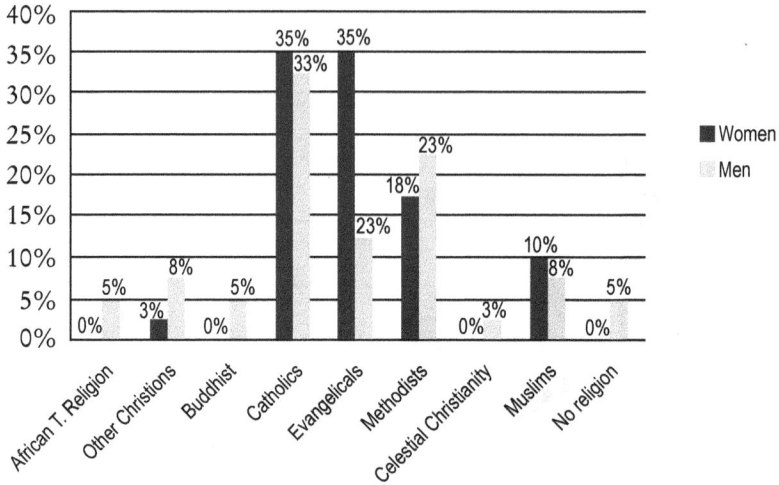

Ethnic affiliation and nationality of spouses. As shown in figure 2.3, 55 percent of couples were of the same ethnicity or ethnic group, and 45 percent were of different ethnic groups. The couples were mainly from the Akan ethnic group (68 percent), followed by the South Mande (11 percent), the North Mande (8 percent), the Krou (6 percent), and the Gur (4 percent). Foreign ethnic groups accounted for 3 percent of the sample. The predominance of the Akan is no surprise because they constitute the largest ethnic group not only in the south of Côte d'Ivoire but also in the city of Abidjan.

According to the provisions of the law, a woman of foreign nationality who marries an Ivorian may acquire Ivorian nationality on the condition that she takes that option at the time of the celebration of the marriage. Foreign male nationals who marry Ivorians may apply for Ivorian nationality two years after the marriage celebration. Of the 240 couples surveyed, 212 couples (88 percent) identified as being of the same nationality. The number of couples who did not have the same nationality was 28, about 12 percent of the sample.

Educational level of spouses. Sixty-three percent of couples surveyed had the same educational level, and 37 percent did not. For couples at the same level, 71 percent had completed some higher education,

Figure 2.3. Ethnicity of spouses

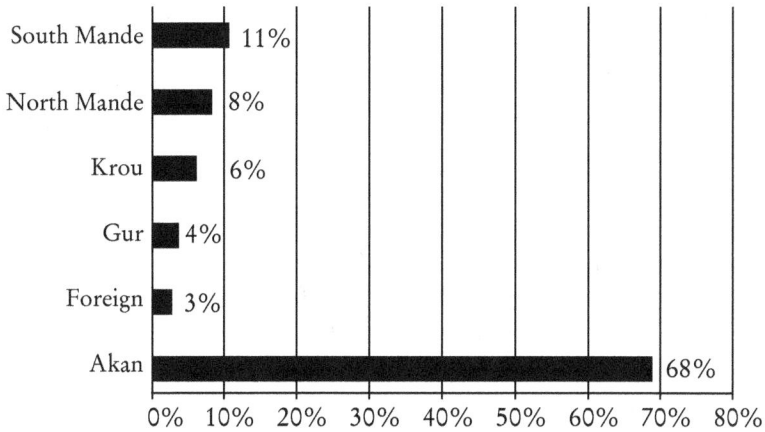

Figure 2.4. Educational level of spouses with the same level of educational attainment

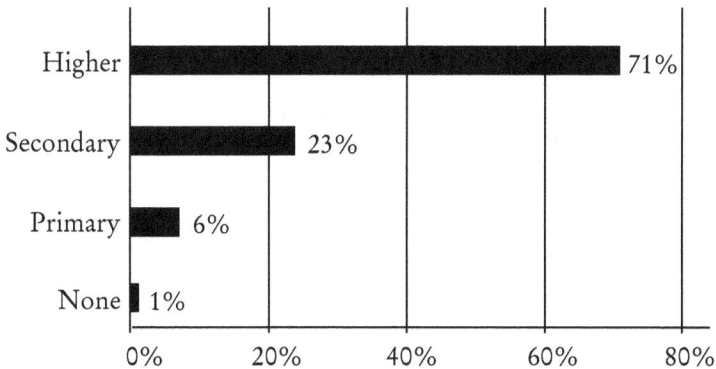

and 23 percent were educated at the secondary level. Those with no education at all or with a primary level of education represented only 1 percent and 6 percent of the sample. The educational attainment of spouses with the same level of education is presented in figure 2.4.

The literacy rate among the population aged fifteen years and older was 43.91 percent in 2014. The enrollment rate in secondary education was 33.41 percent for women and 44.51 percent for men in 2016. For higher education, it was 7.51 percent for women and 10.78 percent for men in 2017 (Unesco Institute for Statistics 2017). The sample collected for this study indicates that 94 percent of those who applied for civil marriage had some higher or secondary education, suggesting a correlation between level of education and interest in civil marriage.

Duration of cohabitation before civil marriage. Figure 2.5 shows that the majority (65 percent) of the couples surveyed were already living together before they applied for civil marriage, while 35 percent were not. Thirty-five percent of cohabiting couples had lived together for up to five years, and 47 percent for a duration of five to fifteen years. Couples who had been cohabiting for fifteen to twenty-five years prior to marriage made up 18 percent of the sample.

It is notable that most couples in Abidjan live together for some time before taking the step of civil marriage despite the fact that many religions, including Christianity and Islam, discourage premarital cohabitation. This seeming contradiction resolves, however, when we consider that for many Muslims, religious marriage is more important than civil marriage. For many Christians, likewise, customary mar-

Figure 2.5. Duration of cohabitation before civil marriage (years)

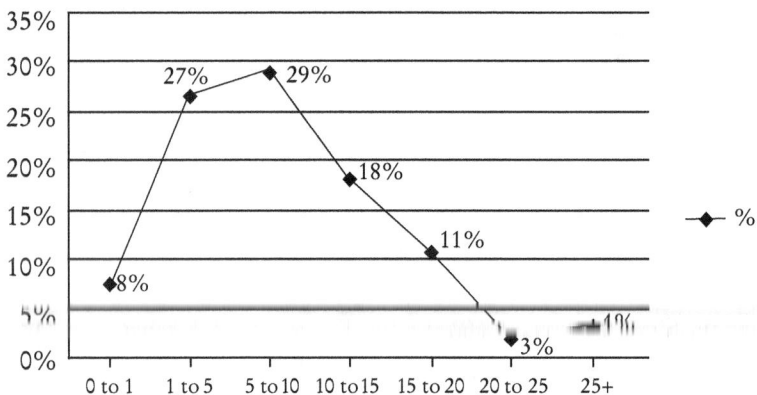

riage is the first required step in the overall process of marriage. This might explain why civil marriage does not seem to be the first priority of many couples.

Customary marriage. Article 20 of the first civil code, Law No. 64–381 of October 7, 1964, abolished the institution of the bride wealth, an injunction accompanied by severe penalties. Thus, in addition to the fact that legal status is granted only to civil marriages in Côte d'Ivoire, the payment of a bride wealth, which symbolizes the materialization of customary marriage in most traditions, is legally prohibited. Nonetheless, 82 percent of couples surveyed admitted to having fulfilled the requirements of customary marriage, including the payment of a bride price, before applying for civil marriage. Among the couples who performed customary marriage, various cohabitation durations were noted: 80 percent of couples had lived together for up to five years before meeting the requirements of their customary marriage, which included saving up the money to pay the bride wealth. Those who lived together five to fifteen years accounted for 16 percent; those who cohabited for more than fifteen years represented 4 percent. Again, these figures demonstrate the resilience of customary marriage despite the legal prohibition of bride price, one of its key factors of legitimation.

In fact, there is no true risk to the persistence of the bride price. Despite the legal prohibition on it and the high penalties, the law is not enforced in any meaningful way. Customary marriages accompanied by exchange of bride wealth might be understood to constitute a form of resistance to state family policies, but this resistance is mild at best, as the illegality of bride price under the law has no real effect on people's decisions about marriage. Everyone, including state and judicial authorities when acting in the private sphere, bows to the unwritten laws of tradition when it comes to using bride price as an instrument of the social legitimation of marriage.

Children from a previous union. Table 2.3 shows that of the 240 couples surveyed, 131 did not have children before marriage. In the remaining 109 couples, one of the spouses had at least one child from a previous union. With regard to dependent children of previous unions, the difference between men and women was not extreme. Seventy-two percent of women did not have dependent children from other unions,

Table 2.3. Participants with children from a previous union

Number	Husband	%	Wife	%
0	154	64	173	72
1	39	16	41	17
2	18	8	12	5
3	14	6	10	4
4	6	3	2	1
5	6	3	2	1
6	1	0	0	0
8	2	1	0	0
	240	100	240	100

compared to 64 percent of men. As more women pursue opportunities in higher education, we see larger numbers of women with no children upon marriage and declining numbers of widowed women with children who are remarrying.

Professional situation of spouses and family income. Recent data suggests that Côte d'Ivoire has a high labor force participation rate of 76.8 percent and a low unemployment rate of 6.7 percent. In rural areas, the labor participation rate reaches 85 percent, versus 68 percent in urban areas. But "only 23 percent of the workers are employed in wage-jobs," and "the remaining 77 percent operate in informal activities such as self-employment on family farms, or selling goods and services" (Saw 2017). Rural residents and women constitute the majority of the self-employed, as 87 percent of employed women are self-employed, compared to 69 percent of employed men.

One striking feature of the data, shown in table 2.4, is the significant number of salaried individuals among the husbands (65 percent) and wives (37 percent). Another is the great proportion of salaried couples. Of those who were not earning a salary, women were the more numerous (39 percent) in comparison to men (29 percent). Despite the new provisions of the marriage law that demand joint management of the household, a small number of women were found to stay at home as housewives (8 percent); no men stayed home. Eight percent of women

Table 2.4. Professional situation of spouses

Professional Situation	Wife Number	%	Husband Number	%
Housewife	18	8	0	0
Jobseeker	19	8	4	2
Pupil	1	0	0	0
Student	21	9	3	1
Non-salaried	93	39	70	29
Salaried	88	37	157	65
Retired	0	0	6	3
TOTAL	240	100	240	100

Note: "Pupil" refers to primary or secondary school level. "Student" refers to higher education levels.

reported they were job seekers, and 9 percent were students, compared to 2 percent and 1 percent of men, respectively. This suggests a correlation between a stable professional situation and the practice of civil marriage, which makes sense, because marriage ceremonies can be costly.

Family income helps determine family financial autonomy. The new provisions of the law speak of common financial management in Article 58. Spouses operate in a framework of both collective and individual responsibility, freedom, and equality, and as a rule, a policy of comanagement of their common life and expenses is expected by the state. Because both Articles 58 and 59 refer to the financial contribution of both spouses, monthly family income was an important consideration in gathering data for this study. Figure 2.6 shows that only 4 percent of the spouses indicated a lack of a stable monthly income. While 22 percent reported monthly income of less than 100,000 FCFA, more than half (64 percent) reported a monthly income ranging from 100,000 to 500,000 FCFA. Just 10 percent of couples reported a monthly income of 500,000 FCFA or more. This data further suggests a relatively strong correlation between the level of income and recourse to marriage under civil law in Côte d'Ivoire.

Figure 2.6. Monthly family income (FCFA)

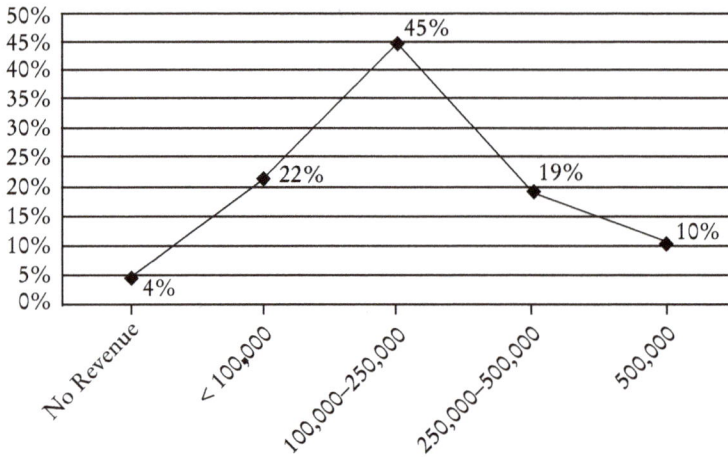

Decisions about estate management. The provisions of the family law of August 2, 1983, unchanged in the 2013 revision, stipulate that "marriage has the effect of creating between the spouses a community of property, unless they expressly opt for the regime of separation of property" (Article 69). Before the marriage ceremony and at the time of completion of the preliminary formalities, such as the filing of documents, spouses freely choose by simple declaration the model of organization and management of their estate. On the day of the celebration of the marriage, the spouses confirm this choice before the registrar and the assembly. It is imperative that the spouses agree on the choice. The survey data shows that the community of property rule is the mode of estate organization and management preferred by Ivorian spouses. Eighty-four percent of the couples surveyed opted for this regime. Only 16 percent opted for the regime of separation of ownership of property.

Already, a survey conducted in 1987, four years after the 1983 revision of family law, revealed that out of 2,595 marriages celebrated, only 167 couples opted for the regime of separation of property (Vléï-Yoroba 1997, 3). If indeed the regime of separation of property is more customary than that of the community of property, as some have argued (2), then the preference for the latter seems to suggest a progressive break from tradition. I argue that concern about the financial and material security of children seems to explain why women tend to prefer the regime of community of property. In the event of the death of the spouse or of divorce, they can legally claim part of the property of the husband to take care of the children. The burden of care for children often falls on women.

Choice of residence. The 2013 family law prescribes that the family domicile is chosen by common consent of the spouses. In case of disagreement, the domicile of the family is fixed by the judge, taking into account the interests of the family. The spouses are co-owners of the lease, which is used exclusively for their dwelling, even if it was signed by only one of them before the marriage (Article 60). Among the Abidjan couples, the proportion who chose their residence together was 86 percent, as opposed to 13 percent of couples whose residence was chosen by the husband alone. Only 1 percent of couples lived in a residence chosen by the wife alone.

The data presented in this section suggests that the practice of civil marriage in Côte d'Ivoire is primarily an urban phenomenon. Indeed, Abidjan alone, the single major city of the country, is home to more than 60 percent of all the civil marriages celebrated in Côte d'Ivoire. Secondly, because civil marriage is expensive, it is affordable only to middle and upper classes. Given the high unemployment rate among the youth in Côte d'Ivoire, more and more young adults are delaying marriage due to financial difficulties. When Ivorians do marry, they tend to marry within the same religion and the same ethnic group. Finally, the data shows that future spouses enjoy more freedom of choice of their marriage partners in a context of declining parental authority.

Marriage in postcolonial Côte d'Ivoire has multiple layers and constraints that most Ivoirians cannot afford either economically or socially. Indeed, while the demand for civil marriage has grown over the years in urban Côte d'Ivoire, it remains a minority practice in the country. Therefore, we cannot expect that the revision of the Ivorian family law will necessarily have brought about changes in marriage practice for the majority of women, especially for rural women.

As illustrated by the practice of marriage in modern Côte d'Ivoire, negotiating modernity in Africa means necessarily negotiating multiplicity and plurality. West African postcolonial societies are immersed in legal, religious, ethnic, and medical plurality. Therefore, negotiating modernity in Africa is about navigating and arbitrating between different spheres of authority, community, and identity.

In the making of African modernity, the modern state inherited from colonialism plays a central role. It seeks to control customary and religious spheres and authorities. But customary and religious authorities have proven to be very ingenious at accommodating, resisting, and even manipulating mechanisms and processes of state control to serve their own interests. In spite of the imposition of civil marriage as the only legal marriage by colonial authorities, both religious and customary marriage, including polygamy and the practice of bride price, have survived and still enjoy strong social legitimacy.

One of the characteristics of the making of African modernity is the fragmentation of the spheres and institutions of social legitimization. Marriage in West African societies is a "total social fact," meaning an activity that has wide-ranging implications in multiple spheres: the customary, the religious, and the secular. Each of these spheres has its own dynamics of identity, community, and authority. Individuals learn how to navigate these multiplicities through doing it. Multiple authorities mean multiple communities and multiple belongings. Identities are fashioned in the interstices of these multiplicities, which can constrain or enhance individual agency depending on the circumstances.

CHAPTER THREE

Religious and Secular Perspectives on Gender Reforms

Five years after the 2013 reform of the family code in Côte d'Ivoire, I conducted qualitative research on its reception in Muslim, Catholic, and secular constituencies in the city of Abidjan. This chapter presents the results of that study. Of importance here are interviewees' perceptions of modernity in connection with the gender reform. The emphasis is on their differentiated understandings of the notion of gender equality and the implications such understandings have for family.

The chapter begins with a reflection on religion and gender in West Africa. Then follows empirical data organized so as to distinguish women's from men's perspectives. A second, generational distinction is made to test whether youth perspectives differ significantly from those of older generations. Two salient points emerge from these interviews, which were conducted five years after the 2012 family code reform in Côte d'Ivoire. First, the interviewees did not reject the notion of gender equality, but understood it differently from how it was presented in the family law reform. Second, the interviewees were nearly unanimous, regardless of their background, on the necessity of a single head of the family, with a clear preference for male leadership.

RELIGION AND GENDER

Religion plays a central role in the construction of gender categories and the legitimation of gender hierarchies (Castelli 2001, 10). Because religions are part of the problem, they should also be part of solutions to gender inequalities. In enacting gender reforms, it is important to be sensitive to what Elizabeth Castelli calls "the ways in which apparently progressive institutional gestures can have unexpected and changeable effects on those whose situations they seek to remedy" (2001, 11).

Linda Woodhead notes that heeding the variable of gender in the sociology of religion is a relatively recent development in a subdiscipline dominated by masculine perspectives (2013, 58; see also Becker 2007; Rochefort and Sanna 2013). She argues: "The second half of the twentieth century has seen important moves within Christianity, Judaism and Islam to consolidate identity around a defense of 'traditional' roles for men and women which involve male headship and female domesticity. Although this tendency is evident across the spectrum of religious commitment—from the more moderate to the more traditionalist—in the former it may be a function of standing still whilst cultural and sexual values liberalize, whilst in the latter there is a more active drive to consolidate highly differentiated and unequal gender roles" (2013, 65).

Although Woodhead acknowledges "[r]eligion's central role in consolidating gender difference and inequality" (2013, 70; see also Portier 2013), her theories of religion and gender include tactical and countercultural types of religious engagement with gender that are more subversive of patriarchal structures. Both Islamic feminism and Christian feminism fall into the category of Woodhead's tactical perspective because they seek to reform patriarchal structures from within by reinterpreting scripture and traditions in ways that challenge male domination (Kwok 2004; Schröter 2017).

In African religious systems, gender dynamics have changed considerably over time as traditional notions were reshaped by colonial discourse and then changed again in the course of independence movements. In some precolonial societies, linguistic analyses show that there were no linguistic gender distinctions, allowing social roles to be filled on the basis of lineage and seniority. In African traditional religions (ATRs), gender was more ambiguously defined and of secondary importance (Hackett 2000, 239). Faith systems, spirit possession, divine symbolism, and religious leadership were open to all regardless of gender, creating a space of power with political, economic, and social sway that was more concerned with religious influence than with gender. Because in ATRs religion is broadly understood as a way to link a community of believers to a sacred spiritual being, there is no inherent restriction on the role of women versus men, but rather a focus on cooperation for mutual fulfillment. Therefore, women were unrestricted in many ways in ATRs from gathering power in the private and public spheres alike. Gender roles were understood more as complementary than as hierarchical (Njoh and Akiwumi 2012, 2–3).

Colonialism in Africa brought new religions with it, fundamentally changing the traditional African ways of life. Islam and Christianity each affected African societies, and scholars still debate whether the influence of these religions was to the detriment or benefit of gender equality. Recent studies have tried to measure these effects; one such attempt involved the Millennium Development Goals, which laid out eight targets in 2000, the third of which was female empowerment. Empowering women, according to these goals, entailed a concerted focus on four target areas: (a) raising the percentage of girls in school, (b) improving female literacy rates, (c) encouraging female employment in nonagricultural sectors, and (d) increasing female representation in government.

When Islam was first introduced to Africa, Muslim actors sought to redefine women's sphere to be less public, in accordance with Islamic doctrine. Similarly, Christian missionaries sought to civilize African societies. Preachers used biblical passages to promote African, and especially female, cultural subordination. This shaped educational systems, which prepared boys for the labor market and girls for life as housewives. A recent progress analysis of the Millennium Development Goals measured the relationship between Christianity, Islam, African traditional religions, and the goals' four target areas to understand how each religion affects gender dynamics (Njoh and Akiwumi 2012). This study found that religion determines a statistically significant portion (22 percent) of variability in women's empowerment. ATRs and

Christianity correspond positively with female participation in nonagricultural activities, and Christianity positively affects female literacy through education. Islam is negatively associated with participation in the nonagricultural sector and literacy rates, as Islam's ideology of female domesticity keeps girls from school and relegates women to the home (16).

These findings, however, cannot account for the entire scope of religion's influence on women's empowerment. In particular, Islam is often misunderstood. Some problematic assumptions regarding women and Islam include the idea that there is a single notion of women's place, that status and problems are identical for all women, and that Islam generally seeks to marginalize women (Frede and Hill 2014, 132). In fact, women in West Africa have improved their lives through Islamic reform movements that emphasize education and through female-led revitalization organizations for Muslims. Men and women increasingly hold formal and informal positions of authority, which both give access to power. Muslim women's experiences are diverse and complex; African women are becoming more visible and active in Islam, yet their morality and bodies continue to be regulated with religious justification (155). Men often have access to power refused to women—and yet this situation makes room for women-only spaces where Muslim women seek to empower themselves. It is helpful, then, when studying Muslim religious communities to pay attention to how religion and gender intertwine, keeping in mind the complexity affecting communities differently and shaping what it means to be a Muslim man or woman.

It is a fact that missionary Christianity and Islam operate within a predominantly patriarchal framework, with governance structures and ideological matrixes that reproduce what Pierre Bourdieu termed "masculine domination" (Bourdieu 2014; Heinen 2013; Ahmed 1992). What is at stake in religion as a prime site for "the construction of gender as well as sexuality" is the control of women's bodies (Della Sudda and Malochet 2012, 30), which are a "significant zone for the inscription of social norms, practices and values" (Pereira and Ibrahim 2010, 921). But some studies have shown how women manage to carve spaces of autonomy in male-dominated religious structures (Della Sudda and Malochet 2012, 31).

After Vatican II, Catholicism generally came to accept "the secularity of the state and of state legislation" and relocated its attention "from state to civil society and the adoption of the discourse of human rights" in the public sphere (Casanova 2017, 49; see also Portier 2005 and Lado 2012). On gender issues, the Catholic church is still uncomfortable with the secularization of state legislation and morality. Yet Casanova argues that the trend is toward consolidation of public opinion in support of the liberalization of sexual mores, especially in the Catholic countries of Europe and Latin America. Increasingly, these states are passing "legislation on family and gender issues, which goes against the publicly asserted official teachings of the church hierarchy, but is supported by public opinion and even the majority of self-defined Catholic population in those countries" (2017, 53; see also Portier and Théry 2015).

In West Africa, on the other hand, public opinion generally follows the views of conservative religious leaders who tend to portray the state and progressive civil society organizations as stooges of the decadent West. In such a context, religious leaders reposition themselves as guardians of traditional values in the public sphere. West Africa has not yet embraced the "radical secularization of the private sphere of individual consciousness" (Casanova 2017, 49) that is being observed in the West. From this perspective, Africa remains a profoundly religious continent (Appleby 2012; Tesfai 2010).

THE IVORIAN RELIGIOUS LANDSCAPE

According to its most recent general population census (which took place in 2014), Côte d'Ivoire's population is estimated at 22.7 million people (Institut National de la Statistique de Côte d'Ivoire 2014). Non-Ivorians account for about 24.2 percent of the general population, making Côte d'Ivoire the most attractive destination of immigrants in the subregion. Immigration heavily shapes the religious landscape of the country. As table 3.1 shows, religious statistics reveal that although Muslims are the majority population in the country, more than half are immigrants from neighboring countries. Thirteen percent of Catholics in the country are non-Ivorians.

Table 3.1. Religious distribution of the Ivorian population

Religion	Ivorians (%)	Non-Ivorians (%)	Percentage of Population
Catholics	18.5	13.0	17.2
Methodists	2.1	0.4	1.7
Evangelicals/ Pentecostals	14.5	3.3	11.8
Celestial Christians	0.5	0.2	0.4
Harrists	0.7	0.0	0.5
Other Christians	2.7	0.8	2.2
Total Christians	39.1	17.7	33.9
Muslims	33.7	72.7	42.9
Traditional Religions	4.4	0.9	3.6
Other Religions	0.6	0.2	0.5
No Religious Affiliation	22.2	8.5	19.1
Total	100.0	100.0	100.0

Source: National Institute of Statistics 2014.

The last three decades in sub-Saharan Africa have been marked by a certain degree of religious liberalization, leading to a boom in religious innovation. Religious pluralism is a major component of the African landscape. This pluralism is expressed not only in the coexistence of many religious traditions within the same country but also in the multiplicity of denominations within religious traditions. Africa is home to three dominant religious traditions—African traditional religions, Islam, and Christianity—which intersect in many ways and influence people's spiritual views (Hanson 2014, 103). Due to the relatively small proportion of Ivorians who practice ATRs, and to the status of Catholics as the largest group of Christians in the country, this chapter deals with the reception of the 2013 family code only in Catholic and Muslim circles.

The history of Christianity in Africa began in North Africa as early as the second century CE, but the practice of this religion has expanded greatly in sub-Saharan Africa only in the past two hundred years, as foreign missionaries and African converts continued to spread their faith. Over time, new African prophets emerged to adapt Christianity to an African context, leading first to African independent churches and then more recently to the rapid growth of Pentecostal and Charismatic churches. Islam was introduced in North Africa in the eighth century CE and quickly spread to West Africa thanks to trans-Saharan trade. West Africa Islam, although today challenged by reformist groups, is still dominated by Sufi orders (Hanson 2014, 121).

According to a 2010 publication of the Pew Forum, there are about 234 million Muslims and 484 million Christians in Africa out of a population of 1.155 billion (Pew Research Center 2010). The remaining third of the population is made up of those who practice traditional religions and members of various esoteric and mystical groups, including pockets of Eastern spiritualty. According to statistical projections, in 2060, 42 percent of the world's Christians and 26 percent of the world's Muslims will be from sub-Saharan Africa (Pew Research Center 2015). But clear-cut statistics can be misleading when it comes to religious practice in Africa due to the complexity of concepts of religious belonging. In sub-Saharan African daily religious practice, religion is perceived and lived primarily as a problem-solving tool. Many believers expect God to solve their social problems, such as finding a spouse, bearing a child, curing an illness, landing a job, fighting witchcraft, and obtaining a visa, especially in the context of the crisis of the social responsibility of the state.

It is apparent that religion as a social force will continue to grow on the continent and influence societal processes. Each of Africa's religions has a unique effect and a different viewpoint on gender roles. Under Islamic law and African customs, for example, men may have multiple wives, and women have different requirements for dress and public presentation depending on which religion dominates. Christianity, on the other hand, generally promotes monogamous marriages, and both men and women have specific behavioral expectations stipulated by the church (Frahm-Arp 2008, 85).

The rich religious history and layered spiritual landscape of Côte d'Ivoire raises interesting questions about how religion mediates Ivorians' interpretation of the revised family code, as well as their understanding of gender equality, marriage, and modernity more generally. The research data presented in the next section delves into contemporary Ivorians' views on these subjects.

METHODOLOGY

Since the revision of the family code in 2013, no social scientific study has focused on the new code's reception among the Ivorian population. This chapter seeks to fill that gap. The qualitative data that forms its foundation was collected from June to September 2016 through semi-structured interviews of individuals and focus groups in eight of the ten municipalities of Abidjan. As the economic capital of Côte d'Ivoire, Abidjan symbolizes cultural heterogeneity and modernity. The study's target population was made up of three categories of actors: Catholic, Islamic, and secular. A total of twenty-eight individual interviews and fourteen focus groups were conducted. The number of people in each focus group ranged from six to twelve participants. Data on participants in individual interviews is presented in table 3.2, and data on focus group composition is presented in table 3.3.

Table 3.2. Professions of participants in individual interviews

Profession	Number
Imam and Islamic leader	5
Catholic priest	5
Mayor	4
Magistrate	1
Lawyer	1
Parliamentarian	1
Notary	1
Social worker	2
Civil society organization leader	2
Leader of ethnic community	6
Total	28

Table 3.3. Composition of focus groups by age, marital status, and gender

	Group Characteristics			Number of Groups
Age and Marital Status of Participants	*Homogeneous Groups*		*Mixed Group*	
	Male	*Female*	*Male + Female*	*Number*
Youth (not married, 18–25 years old)	1	1	1	3
Adult (married, 25 years or older)	1	1	1	3
Total	2	2	2	6

Note: Twelve focus group discussions (six among Catholics and six among Muslims) were conducted in the city of Abidjan. For each religion, the criteria detailed above were used to form the groups.

Composition of the focus groups took into account not only religious belonging but also the age (generation), marital status, and gender of participants. In addition, two group discussions were conducted with control groups of young people and adults from other religions or without affiliations. The interviews focused on the participants' perceptions of modernity, marriage, and the new marriage law. The aim of the focus groups was to stimulate debate in order to examine consensus and contradictions on the issues, so that recurrences could be identified from participants' responses.

The interviews were conducted with religious leaders, community leaders, and participants from private and public institutions (magistrates, lawyers, notaries, mayors, social workers), as well as civil society actors in charge of family and matrimonial matters. The interviews had a semi-structured format around the following topics: (a) perceptions and social representations of modernity, marriage, and family; (b) normative and institutional frameworks of marriage and the family; and (c) roles, statuses, and social relationships within families. The data revealed that for secular study participants (magistrates, lawyers, parliamentarians, notaries, social workers, mayors, leaders in civil society, and community leaders), there is a wide distance between the new code and the interview subjects' religious beliefs.

EMPIRICAL DATA

Women's perspectives

Married Catholic women (MCW). The married Catholic women interviewed described modernity in terms of social changes and transformations. These changes are seen as part of the evolution of attitudes and practices, and they can be either positive or negative. Some of the positive aspects of modernity these women cited include openness to the world, rapid sharing of knowledge, and the many forms of exchange. Negative aspects include the neglect of basic childhood education, excessive focus on material goods, corruption of the human conscience, rise of internet marriages, increase in divorce, promotion of homosexuality, and decline of belief in God. Common themes can be seen in the following interview excerpts:

> For me, modernity is the fact that life revolves around money; it is a life of selfish interest. (MCW 1)

> I can say that modernity is the lack of religious and familial following. It is also the development of technology, a lack of belief in God, convenience, the evolution of young girls' behavior tied to the pursuit of easy gain, that is to say, greed, which manifests itself through the refusal to pursue education, to work. I must add to this, the mastery of computer-based skills by children as compared to their parents. (MCW 2)

> People have turned from the traditional norms of our days. Modernity has taken the upper hand within our couples. This is at the root of divorces. There is no longer a belief in God. (MCW 3)

Married Catholic women interviewees categorically and unanimously rejected homosexuality, which they linked to the perversion of modernity. These women deplore the resignation to homosexuality of some parents and the state, which, in their opinion, does not do enough to combat what they see as a scourge for humanity. With modernity, homosexuality is gaining ground, a development contrary to the wishes of God. Thus, modernity is understood by the married Catholic women as having a perverse rather than a positive effect, because it has eroded traditional social values. Based on cultural traditions and Christianity, these women define marriage in terms of a union between a man and a woman:

> With evolution, homosexual marriage, for example, which in the past was a clandestine and rare practice, is now widespread as something normal, to the point that we vote on laws to legalize this abominable practice. (MCW 3)

> I return to the question of homosexuality: the Bible said that man will leave his father and mother and attach himself to a woman. This is to say that marriage is between a man and a woman and not between two individuals of the same sex. (MCW 5)

Regarding the reception of the new legal provision on marriage, the married Catholic women, who admitted having only a vague understanding of it, summarized these laws in terms of equality between men and women in the household. But some noted that the Bible subordinates woman to man, not that she might be a slave, but that the two might complete each other. These Catholic women affirmed that the new law was not needed, and they understood the notion of equality promoted by the law as a source of disorder and conflict in the family. For them, a woman's role is to contribute to the well-being of the family and not to "wear the pants" at home. They support equality on the professional level but reject it on the domestic level, characterizing it as contrary to Christianity and to African traditions. "We cannot have two captains in the same ship," one explained. Other comments on the laws about marriage included the following:

> For me, I do not find that this new law concerns a normal family. The man must remain the man, and the woman must know her place in the home. Otherwise, this law will give wings to women.

The woman must instead help the man. But to say that we are equal, I deplore this context. (MCW 6)

In my opinion, the man being the master, it is he who must meet the needs of the family. But the woman must always lend him aid. (MCW 3)

As for me, I can say that the roles of husband and wife must be complementary. Because both are educators first. But it is the man who is in charge of the family. Education falls on both, but principally it is the duty of the woman. (MCW 6)

I think the creation of this article [of the family law] stems from the fact that the majority of women do not participate in family spending decisions despite the considerable revenue available to them. Thus, this article seeks to establish harmony within the couple. (MCW 4)

We say that before God I do not have the right to prosecute my husband. But I will say instead, I must always communicate with him to find a middle ground before making any decision. It is crucial that we understand each other in the family. (MCW 5)

With modernity, man and woman have the same rights on an intellectual level. Thus, he cannot impose a profession on his wife. (MCW 4)

Married Catholic women believe that the man must ensure familial care, ensure the supervision of the family, and play the role of decision maker for the good of the family. The woman must oversee the children's education, provide affection to the children, ensure the children's success, and take care of her husband. The Catholic women interviewed are unanimous in their belief that, despite the law, men must remain the heads of families and women should support them.

Young, single Catholic women (YSCW). Young, unmarried Catholic women also have an ambivalent perception of modernity, which they associate with the notion of change. These changes are linked to the development and emergence of new communication and information technologies. Concerning positive aspects of modernity, they noted the appearance of new technologies, education, and openness to the wider world. Negative aspects of modernity include moral depravation, the progression of homosexuality, parents' laxity in educating their children, and the insubordination of women in the household.

These young women linked their perceptions of marriage to their religious beliefs as well as to their cultural traditions. They defined marriage in terms of a union between a man and a woman and rejected the idea of homosexual marriage. They assigned no worth to homosexuality because they believe that a woman's value derives from her experience of childbirth. They consider acceptance of homosexuality to be something that the West wants to impose on Africa.

The young Catholic women expressed familiarity with the reform of the marriage law but not with the details. They were aware that the reform concerns gender equality: the woman must assume the same roles as the man in the family. For them, this new law must be seen as a source of motivation for women who rely solely on men in a marriage: it is a means to allow the woman to be more responsible. Some young Catholic women expressed a belief, however, that to speak of equality might exacerbate women's insubordination and lead to conflicts within the family.

Like the married Catholic women, the single women expressed approval of gender equality in terms of education and at the level of professional integration, but they also do not value equality within marriage. They suggested that the state should further publicize the law, clarifying the notion of equality through awareness campaigns. On the subject of the allocation of familial roles, their choice of metaphors is revealing: young, single Catholic women see men as the "president of the family," "decision maker," "governor," and "caretaker of the family." The woman is "vice-president," "educator of children," "consultant in the family," and "assistant of the family." As the following excerpts show, young Catholic women are unanimous on that it is the man who is head of the family:

What I know about this new law is the following: man and woman are both head of the family and are charged with bearing family expenses together. It is a law seeking to motivate the woman to work with and support her husband. And not only in completing household chores. This law leads the woman to no longer hold out her hand to the man to beg. This law raises a woman's awareness and empowers her. Also, due to this law, there is no longer respect between a woman and her husband. Because she is obliged to put her hand in her own pocket. (YSCW 4)

For me, this law will empower some men to exaggerate in seeking to know the salary of their wives and force them to share in household expenses in an equitable manner. That might be a source of conflict at home. (YSCW 5)

This new law is of more concern to couples where both spouses work. It can cause men to impose certain burdens on women. The woman's duty is to support her husband and not to impose any burdens on him. If not, she risks taking over and becoming authoritarian in the home. It is this aspect that I deplore. (YSCW 6)

I do not agree with equality within the couple because it drives the woman to no longer submit to her husband. Women must be allowed to be well-rounded but not in charge in the same sense as the man in the home, because having economic power is not synonymous to women's authority and insubordination in the home. She must always recognize her place and her position in the home. Therefore, for me, equality between man and woman is that the two can apply themselves to the same tasks professionally but not within the home. On this question of equality, I hope to see an awareness campaign throughout the country. (YSCW 7)

Equality is good, because that will bring an advantage to the home. But the woman must remain subordinate to her husband. If not, it will discredit her spouse. It is while the man is not there that the woman must become head of the family. As the Bible says, a woman must submit to her husband because it is from him that she was created. This goes to say that man already existed before woman. Therefore, woman must not defy man. On a throne, it is only man who sits there. Woman is complementary. It is man who makes decisions, and woman follows. I must also say that this law concerns couples where both spouses work. (YSCW 8)

Man is like the president, and woman is the vice president and the man's advisor. The man governs the house, and the woman supports him. Each completes the other with advice and with the children's education. The Bible says, Woman, submit to your husband; it is he who is head of the family. Moreover, when God created humans, he first created man and then made woman from man, having seen the solitude that so bothered him. (YSCW 9)

Interviews revealed more convergences than divergences between married Catholic woman and young, unmarried Catholic women. Both expressed similarly ambivalent views of modernity to which they attributed the perversion of morals, rejected homosexuality in favor of a heterosexual norm, and presented a nuanced and complementary vision of the equality of man and woman. Above all, both maintained the importance of the man's authority within the family. This shared outlook on relations between men and women in marriage is both a religious and traditional cornerstone. However, the young women appear more receptive than the married women to equality in educational and professional domains. Equality in these contexts is understood more in the sense of a reinforcing complementarity than in creating a distinction in family roles.

Married Muslim women (MMW). Married Muslim women associated modernity with both positive and negative changes in society, including a growing lack of respect for religious and traditional clothing norms, the introduction of new communication technologies, climate change, their children's freedom of spousal choice, the end of corporal punishment as a tool for teaching children, the legal recognition of children in cases of adultery, the valorization of children's rights, children's growing disobedience, and homosexual marriage. Illustrative comments about modernity included the following:

Men and women dress in a manner unworthy of religion. Thus, on this basis, God punishes us, as illustrated by current events. (MMW 1)

Today, children oppose their parents' choices; before, children did not do so. The child says that he has rights. What rights? It is modernity. (MMW 2)

Before, arranged marriages succeeded better than marriages do now, and things went well because daughters did not disobey their parents. (MMW 3)

In Muslim law, adultery is forbidden. The law today recognizes children born out of wedlock. Often, even, the child can hold you legally accountable. (MMW 5)

With regard to all these changes, married Muslim women expressed a view of modernity as a factor in social change that causes social imbalance, the loss of parental authority over children, the contradiction of religious norms, and moral depravity.

Married Muslim women understand marriage as a union between a man and a woman. Like their Catholic counterparts, these women categorically reject homosexuality, which they see as contrary to Islam and dangerous for society, perhaps even for health. Homosexuality, here associated with modernity, is viewed as a malediction that incites God's anger:

In Islam, to be married, the man and woman must consent, their parents must give their blessing, but more importantly, the two people must love each other. Then there is the dowry to pay, and once it is paid, the two are married. (MMW 6)

Legal marriage is used to augment the salary of Mr. or Mrs. in order that the children are paid for. (MMW 10)

Homosexual marriage is not permitted by God; God did not ordain that. It is the greatest sin. (MMW 7)

It is modernity that has brought about these homosexual practices. Modernity is a life of debauchery. (MMW 9)

Regarding the new provisions of the marriage law, married Muslim women also admitted not knowing much about them. They explained the law as, among other things, a tool for promoting equality between men and women, a tool for emancipating women, a factor in redefining roles in the family, a violation of Islamic norms, a cause of female disobedience, and a source of marital discord. Some of these views read:

The law speaks of equality between man and woman. (MMW 8)

With this law, we share expenses, yet the Quran states that it is the man who must take care of the woman. (MMW 4)

If the woman agrees to the sharing of duties, all is well in the household. If not, everything worsens. (MMW 6)

The woman will speak before her husband. It is not normal. (MMW 2)

They are not equal. If your husband speaks, you must not speak; it is he who married you. You do not say anything; you let him speak. The duty of the wife is to respect the husband. Respecting a man also educates the children. (MMW 5)

Concerning the distribution of roles in the family, the married Muslim women interviewees, more than their Catholic counterparts, explained that it is the duty of the man as leader to provide for the material needs of the family. The woman does the housework and ensures the children's education:

The woman is the guardian of the house; she cleans, takes account of all that happens in the house, and educates the children. (MMW 3)

It is the man who must take care of his wife. If she wants to contribute, she can. God says you contribute if you want. Islam is clear on this, but within the law, one is obligated to do so. (MMW 2)

It is shameful for the husband to send his wife before the tribunals to say that she does not contribute to household expenses; in this case, I stopped working, because the woman is not obligated to work in Islam. (MMW 1)

Married Muslim women are aware, however, of the gap between the ideals upheld by religion and the reality within families. They admit that not all men are up to their obligations as prescribed by Islam, making the woman the de facto pillar of the family:

> Sometimes the man puts the burden of food on the woman; Muslim men are somewhat mean. They feebly participate in household expenses. (MMW 9)

> In marriage, all rests upon the woman. If you are married, you are obligated to do all that the man says. If not, your children will not succeed. Thus, women are constrained; too many quarrels between man and woman act on the future of the children. If we are not subordinate, our children leave. They become microbes, grazers. (MMW 10)

> The only thing man cares about is to provide money for daily sustenance, but other expenses are not his problem. If the woman does not participate in the finances, if she is not submissive, it affects the future of children. (MMW 7)

Married Muslim women pointed to their concern for children's well-being as one of the determining factors of the submission of women to masculine authority—hence the importance of finances in family power relations.

Young, single Muslim women (YSMW). Young, single Muslim women also talked about modernity as a social evolution that manifests itself in changes of clothing styles, demands of equality in marriage, more liberty in choosing a marriage partner, more freedom of expression and choice for women, changes in the education of children, developments in the nuclear family, less submission of women to men, homosexual marriage, and rises in divorce.

They perceive some of these changes as positive, especially those related to more freedom for women. But they decry other changes as negative, including what they describe as the increasing popularity of promiscuous clothing and the acceptance of homosexuality. Indeed, using religious references, young, single Muslim women underlined the sacred nature and importance of marriage and invoked the heterosexual norm to reject homosexuality.

The young, single Muslim women, like married Muslim women, were unfamiliar with the details of the family law's new provisions. Some mentioned the contribution of the spouses to family expenses. According to this interview group, the new legal provisions render wives more active, responsible, and autonomous and make husbands participate more in chores. But these young women do not agree with the obligatory participation of women in household expenses. Furthermore, they expressed the belief that the law contradicts Islamic norms, aggravates the insubordination of women, and is a source of conflicts.

With regard to the distribution of roles within the family, the young, single Muslim women expressed unanimous agreement that the man must remain head of the family. In their view, the man, as head of the family, provides for the family's needs. The woman is a support for her husband. She educates the children, advises her husband, and maintains the household:

> It is the man who is head of the family, because it is he who married the woman, who takes care of the house. (YSMW 11)

> The man is head of the family. He is in charge of most family expenses. (YSMW 2)

> In the house, the man mostly takes care of the rent, the food. The man meets the needs of the family. The woman educates the children. (YSMW 6)

> The woman educates the children, supports her husband. The man works but asks his wife about household activities, and he acts in support. The woman advises her husband, comforts him. (YSMW 8)

> The man is head of the family. It is he who pays the dowry according to tradition. In Islam, it is the man who is head of the family. It is he who does all the expenditures. (YSMW 10)

It is clear from the above statements that Muslim and Catholic women in Abidjan, for reasons both cultural and economic as well as religious, do not question the position of men as head of the family. These women advocate for a complementarity of man and woman, with man as head of the family and woman as his aid, advisor, educator of the children, and home keeper.

Professional women. The women interviewed for this section included a notary, two female social workers, and the president of an organization specializing in issues of children, women, and the family. Social workers are employed in the justice system to counsel troubled couples. Of interest here is their professional status, not primarily their religious convictions. The results show that professional status and religious convictions are difficult to separate in the context of Côte d'Ivoire.

The notary. On the subject of the juxtaposition and possible hierarchy of customary, religious, and civil marriages, the female notary opted for a professional posture: "Me, I am an official, and thus the most important marriage is civil marriage, which determines the rights and obligations of the spouses. But there are steps to follow. The precondition to civil and religious marriages is customary marriage." Customary marriage, in her view, "is a sign, an act that pays homage to the families."

On the subject of the new legal provisions on marriage, the notary said: "There is no major change. The only most notable change is that parental power is shared by the father and the mother." About her opinion of these new provisions, she affirmed: "I admit that I have not mastered the new law. I only work on the articles concerning parental power and common acts that I handle in my office."

As for the weight she gives to the concept of equality between men and women, she responded: "We do not speak of equality because we are not competing; it is a relationship of two beings who love each other. The law implies an equality, whereas in the physical relationship, there is an inequality that exists naturally between man and woman. It is thus a relationship of complementarity necessary for achieving stability within the couple."

The remarks of the notary about the concept of equality show that she understands it more in terms of complementarity. On the question of the distribution of roles within the family, moreover, she explained her approach as consensual, without departing from the law: "The role of men or women is to meet their commitments regarding the law. Thus, the spouses decide together the role of each. Also, the man is the umbrella, the guardian, the protection. The man has a great mission."

On the issue of who should be the head of the family, she disagrees with the law: "Naturally, it is the man." Regarding shared decision-making concerning residence, she laments:

> This clause truly weakens the institution of marriage. For our level of development, we do not need this clause. It is misused by some people and this gives rise to numerous legal disputes which result in many divorces. In general, it is the man who marries the woman; thus, it is the man who chooses the couple's residence. Because, after marriage, it is the woman who goes to the man's home.

Voiced by a female legal expert, this critical position with regard to some new provisions of the Ivorian family code suggests that the professional status or the educational level is not sufficient to obtain women's approval of a feminist legal reform deemed to be progressive and destined to improve the condition of women in society.

Social worker 1 (marriage counselor). On what she knew about the modification of the family code, she responded: "What I know about this new marriage law is that each of the spouses must contribute to the needs of the family in proportion to their salary or earnings. Concerning the management of the children, the parental authority that was previously reserved exclusively for the father has been revised. Now, it is in the hands of the two parents." On the opportunity of this reform, she said: "Personally, this law has never bothered me. Because I already know that when you live in together, you must pull together. Thus, from the moment when you know it, you continue to live as before." Her response suggests that the new law need not be understood as revolutionary. She continued: "This is [a] new way of empowering women in the family. The new law upgrades the woman." But, like the notary, she declined to say if the law has negative aspects: "I do not know the law in its entirety, so I cannot judge it."

On the notion of equality in marriage, this social worker made several important distinctions:

> That depends on the meaning that each couple gives to its marriage. I know that, already with my physical constitution, I am not identical to my husband. This is where lies the first difference. On

the financial level, it could happen that I am more at ease financially than my husband, but that does not bother me. The most important thing is that we live in harmony. I am certain equality between man and woman is impossible. Now, in the responsibility that each of us holds, we can sit down to discuss and, depending on our earnings, we will reconsider household expenses. The Catholic religion states that man must provide for the welfare of his wife, of his family. At the same time, Catholicism says that the woman must submit to her husband. However, with their respective inputs, the two must complement each other. According to our customs, the man is head of the family, and the woman is relegated to the background. She does not have the right to speak in an assembly in the presence of men. But according to the law, they are equal.

It is noteworthy that Catholicism is referred to in her interpretation of the notion of equality between men and women. All the distinctions she makes, which privilege complementarity, aim to show that there are domains where men and women will never be equal.

On the subject of the head of the family, she said: "According to me, it is man who is head of the family. This is guaranteed by religion and by our local customs. But according to the law, there is a coresponsibility in family management."

Social worker 2 (marriage counselor). Her assessment of the impact of the family code revision seemed somewhat mixed: "I think people applauded this law when it first arrived, but now we do not know if it is welcomed. We see lots of divorce cases because there is no longer enough respect in the family." She reaffirms the man's authority: "I do not necessarily say that it is bad, but each must at least respect the person across from him or her. Each must do his or her share of things, all while acknowledging the authority of the man." She explained that the risk of these new legal provisions is "disobedience to the husband." Indeed, she is very critical of the notion of equality:

Equality between men and women today is not truly welcome, because we see a lot of divorces. According to religion, you must recognize the man as your spouse. Also, there is no equality between the man and the woman. I prefer this, because at least there is someone who is stronger than the other. According to our customs, man is before woman; at least we know who the head of the family is. I prefer this. When the law says that we are equal, I think that is too strong, because that does not work everywhere.

She also insisted on complementarity, but without hesitation she affirmed, "In my opinion it is man who is head of the family, because he is the authority of the family."

Lawyer. Concerning the revision of the family code, the lawyer is one of the very few who demonstrated familiarity with its content:

In fact, it is not about a new law, but rather about four provisions that were modified. The paragraph that says that the husband is head of the family has been eliminated. From now on, the spouses contribute in equal part to the family expenses. For the wife who does not want to live with her husband, a judge can decide the location of the couple's residence. Before, we would say that the woman must follow her husband.

Invited to give her opinion on the importance and the scope of these modifications, the lawyer responded: "I do not see too much importance in these changes. These new provisions are not explained to the population. They are applied poorly. The initiators must raise awareness of the basics of this law." When asked about the aspects of the revision that she judges problematic, she affirmed: "The change that struck me most is the fact of omitting the paragraph on the head of the family. . . . We are not yet ready to accept that we are in an organization without a head. That bothers me, because it is poorly considered." This interviewee suggested that Ivorian society is not prepared for this modification that creates more problems than it resolves.

On the concept of equality, she made the same differentiation as the second social worker, drawing on cultural traditions, religion, or law:

[The new family law] makes man and woman equal as much as possible, notably, on the level of treatment within society and of employment. But on the religious level, there is a certain equality, because the church considers us all children of God. Now, the inequality is found in the fact that women cannot be Catholic priests. Women cannot perform mass or confession. At the customary level, there is no equality, because in our traditions men are different from women. Women do not speak before their husband. Finally, at the legal level, the law tries to place husband and wife on the same footing.

The lawyer articulated her opinion on the distribution of familial roles in these terms: "The role of the man in marriage is to serve as a guide, a marker, and a model for the family. He must bring in money for the family. He must not be someone who talks too much, but someone who says useful things. The woman is truly the assistant. She must pay attention to details. In conclusion, the man is the brain of the family, and the woman is the heart." But for her, it does not follow that man is automatically head of the family, a term she associates with responsibility: "The head of the family is someone who behaves like a man, that is to say, who is responsible. Someone who fights for the well-being of the family. Thus, the head can be the man, just as the woman can be the head, too."

President of the NGO ONEF (the National Organization for Children, Women, and the Family). The president of ONEF's administrative council put the novelty of the family code revision in relative terms: "This happened already even without the code. The code has not changed everyday household activities. Society has attributed roles to men and to women, and that is what functions." She believes the law has not been applied with sensitivity, and in fact that its adoption was motivated by the desire "to get Millennium funds." On the question of the head of the family, she referred to religion: "In reference to religion, the man is head of the family because it is he who leaves his family to unite with a woman in order to form a single flesh." However, "the true power is the woman's": "officially, the man is the head; unofficially, it is the woman who is the head." She, too, privileges complementarity over equality: "Man and woman are complementary. The woman prepares the food and cleans. The man produces the money."

The reforms relative to gender equality primarily seek to improve women's condition in society. The interviews revealed that even if women believe in the importance of advancing equality in terms of fundamental human rights (education, professional life, health, participation in economic life, and so forth), they continue to understand equality in the domestic sphere in terms of complementarity or dialogue between the man and the woman.

Men's perspectives

Married Catholic men (MCM) and *young, single Catholic men (YSCM)* share the same views on gender equality. For this reason, unlike with the data on Catholic and Muslim women, they are not treated separately. These men accept modernity as a good thing insofar as it improves the conditions of daily life through scientific, medical, and technological progress. They see it as a tool for well-being, an opportunity for the emancipation of women and of children, and a way to aspire to greater freedom. Catholic men expressed some reservations, however, about the adoption of modernity, and they rejected certain practices that they attribute to modernity—namely, moral depravity and the legitimization of behaviors they believe breach local sociocultural values.

What dominates these perceptions of modernity, as in the interviews with the women, is its ambivalence—the largely shared idea that modernity has both positive and negative aspects. The negative aspects are attributed to an excess of freedom and often fall under the domain of morality. Concerning marriage, for example, several interviewees expressed with regret that they see marriage like a contract, a game of interests, an engagement determined by strategies of economics, professionalism, social prestige, and conformity, more than as a relationship based on love. For the interviewees, marriage is moving away from the fundamentals that make up a divine institution. From a religious perspective, the interviewees defined marriage as a contract that unites a man and a woman. They described marriage as having sacramental value, entailing responsibility to procreate and sustain society and the family.

As for homosexuality and homosexual marriage, the interviewees opposed both. In their view, marriage is a free and informed union between a man and a woman, a divine rather than human institution, and a source of benediction with the goal of procreation. From this standpoint, marriage is incompatible with homosexuality, which they understand as a human creation, a union against nature, a deviant practice that goes against faith, and an abomination. The interview excerpt that follows makes this point:

Now there is a form of legalization of these deviant practices. When you speak of homosexuality, these practices were not legal. They were done in the shadows; we will say it like that. But now I think that with modernity and the debauchery of this new era, these practices have become legal. All the world can go about doing anything. (YSCM 8)

Catholic men, young and old, recognize the importance of the three types of marriage (customary, religious, and civil) and resist the idea of putting them in a hierarchy, believing that each of these types of marriage carries a specific logic of legitimation. They understand customary marriage as uniting two families, civil marriage as a legal recognition by the state, and religious marriage as a cornerstone of divine blessing.

With regard to their knowledge of the provisions of the new marriage law, the interviewees acknowledged having heard of the changes but did not know much about the details. They particularly mentioned that the law promotes equality between men and women as head of the household.

The aspect of the law that interviewees most accepted was the shared management of the household. The aspect interviewees found problematic was the one pertaining to equality between men and women that confers upon the woman the status of one of the heads of the household. Unanimously, the interviewees agreed that only man is head of the family and saw it a divine prerogative. Despite women's recognized virtues and professional and intellectual competencies, the interviewees did not see women as equal to men. Therefore, the woman cannot be head of the family except in cases of the man's absence or of the incapacity of the man to fill his social role as head of the family. The following exchanges from one focus group illustrate these viewpoints:

Yes! As far as what I know [about the new law], it is a marriage where the legislature wished to further gender rights; that is to say, to have the husband and wife at the same level of equality. Contrary to what God says or the church declares that man is head of the family, the two spouses are head of the family. The choice of family residence is carried out by the two, decisions are made together. (MCM 1)

This new law is dangerous. It is a transition toward "marriage for everyone" (*marriage pour tous*), including homosexuals. That is the purpose. In the name of a certain liberty, they want to make you accept that man and woman are equal and have the same rights. Even in society, there are leaders. (MCM 5)

It is as if in a boat, there a several captains; it is a law that sends us all straight into chaos. If already two people dispute leadership, who is there to maintain the discipline and ensure the growth of the children? That is the question I ask myself. Do we have to copy what happens in New York? They have their history, we have ours. There is a need for further thought. And moreover, it is often without consulting us. Our so-called legislators get up and pass laws without truly consulting the population. (MCM 4)

With regard to the question of who is or should be the head of the family, Catholic men, both older and younger, unanimously believe that it is the man.

The two have a joint responsibility; but the man is the boss. (MCM 5)

When the man is present, it is the man who is head. You cannot have two bosses. (MCM 2)

Likewise, both men and women of the younger generations agree that the head of the family remains the man. The following excerpts from the mixed focus group of young Catholic women and men illustrate the point:

It is the man, because it is he who takes care of all the household, the child's education, market transactions, the home; thus, it is normal that we must name him head of the family. (YCM 1)

It is not because we speak as Catholics; God himself said from the beginning it is man who is head of the family, and that is what religions have adopted. Thus, I think that if the man is no longer to be head of the family, God must come tell us that the man is no longer head of the family, and then we will accept it. (YCM 3)

From the perspective of married Catholic men, the new law has not been adapted to local realities, to local customs, or to the church's vision of marriage—and the consequence is the crisis in the family. These men are concerned about future generations. They see a transposition and a legitimation of marital practices already accepted in Western countries and suspect the new reforms will prepare people's mindsets for the eventual acceptance of homosexual marriage. Catholic interviewees use economic, religious, and pragmatic arguments that display a strong internalization—on the part of men as well as women, younger generations as well as older—of practices of socialization in which the father figure is the symbol of familial authority.

Married Muslim men (MMM) and young, single Muslim men (YSMM). The perceptions of Muslim men, both older and younger, on the subject of modernity are not substantially different from those of Christian men, but Muslims refer more often to the Quran as foundation of their opinions than Christians with regard to the Bible. One of the interviewees explains: "I think that, for us Muslims, what the prophet has said is what we follow. We do not even have the right to remove something. It is our prophet; thus, it is he whom we follow" (MMM 1). The following excerpts from a focus group of married Muslim men illustrate well the convergence of Muslim and Catholic men's viewpoints on the family code revision:

Me personally, I have heard about these laws that were voted upon in the assembly. I have heard that they have voted on a new law which gives more rights to women. That is to say, the equality of the sexes. And I have also heard that they voted upon a law that, for example, if you are homosexual, there is no problem. Those are the two laws I know. (MMM 2)

The law of which I speak says that there is gender equality between the man and the woman; in Africa, the man always remains head of the family no matter what. With this law, we return to modernization. There is no longer respect. (MMM 3)

The prophet said that we should not mistreat women because they are our partners—to take good care of women. Now, if today we interpret this poorly, it will lead us to speak of gender equality, whereas in reality the prophet did not speak of gender equality. That is my worry. Gender equality — it is we ourselves who make it, thus to banish what the prophet has said. Thus, I do not agree with it. The prophet has not said that the woman is our slave. Never! What he has said is written; we cannot erase it. But we must not interpret [it] as gender equality. (MMM 5)

Even the people who speak to you of homosexuality, even them, they are born of a woman. That woman united herself with a man. If they are homosexuals, they will marry between themselves, woman-woman, man-man, how will they make children? They will look for children in orphanages. (MMM 6)

That is to say that a woman is an inferior being compared to the man. But in the family you must know that when you are in a boat, there are not two chiefs. There must be a manager. The woman should imagine the family as a business, of which the man is perhaps the President of the Board of Governors and the woman is the CEO. That's how it works. But we cannot say both are on equal footing. Some women have misunderstood it. (YSMM 10)

The interviewees used the Quran as the basis to reject the notion of equality between men and women and to highlight heterosexuality as normative. But some interviewees, as the following excerpt shows, are of the opinion that if there is a concern about the equality of man and woman, it is because men do mistreat women:

Sincerely, we must say the truth. Often what we say, it is not what happens. Often, the husband does not even know what the child eats. He abandons the children, it is the woman who takes care of them. Often, even, he does not even leave money. It is the woman who goes to the market, who sells goods to take care of the family, including the man. It is here you see women at the market. When you look today, it is the woman who is in charge of everything. Whereas God himself says that if woman has paid for meat to put in the sauce, and you eat, you will go directly to Hell. I do not know how to say it, well, it is a sin. But when you look today, it is the woman who pays for school, it is she who takes care of everything. (MMM 6)

On the subject of the distribution of household roles, one idea was predominant in the interviewees' comments: that the woman must principally occupy herself with domestic affairs, while the man must go out to look for the means of taking care of his family:

The woman remains at home, she must take care of the household; first she must make children and then take care of them. She must cook for the family. Now the man, his duty is also to educate the children. It is the man who must go out to work. It is he who gives money to the woman to be able to attend to the needs of the family. (MMM 8)

It is the man who must take care of everything. Even a millionaire woman must not, in any way, be in charge of the household. (MMM 10)

I am not the one saying it. It is written in the Holy Quran. It is man who is the boss. It is written in the Quran. That is why it is the husband who must give money to the wife, to do this or to do that. And it is he who must take care of everything. If she brings money from outside and gives [it to] you, you must refuse. You must take care of her, because that is what God has said in the Holy Quran. (MMM 11)

Let's talk about equality. I do not see equality, as for example the woman has 2 percent and the man has 2 percent. Equality here is to agree on what you have to do. That's equality. It is not that the woman has to pay electricity and I have to pay for water. In a family there is a leader. Now the term "leader" is not a question of domination but of responsibility. What I meant to say is that equality here does not mean equal parts. It's not that. It's a question of responsibility. Each one must know his position. The woman must know that it is she who must cook; the man for example must know that it is he who must give the money for the meal. Equality is not "I pay the electricity bill and you pay the water bills." No! (YSMM 7)

Compared to Catholic men, Muslim interviewees demonstrated less flexibility on the financial contribution of the woman to household expenses. Whereas the Catholic men were more open to a sharing of financial expenses between the man and the woman when both have income generating activities, Muslim men were more affirmative about man's monopoly of financial responsibility in the household, which suggests that among Muslim men, financial responsibility is the basis of masculine authority in the household.

Religious leaders: Catholic priests and imams. Beginning with the priests, the interviews revealed that these religious leaders' knowledge of the new provisions of the Ivorian family code was weak. The following example illustrates the general pattern of comments: "Concerning the law, I am not very knowledgeable and thus cannot respond. For questions of law, you must see a jurist. I have heard about these legal provisions, but I do not know their content. But you need a legal expert in order to properly dissect them; I will speak to you as a pastor" (Catholic priest 2).

Concerning equality between men and women, one Catholic priest distinguished between equality in human dignity, which is common to all humanity, and functional equality in the framework of marriage, which, according to them, is neither biblical nor pragmatic:

It is said in Ephesians 5, "Woman, submit to your husband because he is the head," and at the same time it is said, "Men, love your wives as yourselves." In all organizations, there is always a certain hierarchy or a certain organization. We cannot all do the same things at the same time. First, for technical reasons and for the sake of efficacy. Always, it is that gender cannot absolutely be the criterion for defining the distribution of roles. But also the Church does not intervene in these norms of the domestic economy. Each couple is free to organize the household as they wish, to make choices that foster their communion. (Catholic priest 1)

The man and the woman are two creatures of God. Thus, when you speak of equality, it is as if there is one who dominates the other. The man is head of the family; it is he who is the protector, and he must love his wife as his wife must love him. They are equal. They bring children to the world, educate them, send them to school, and nurture them. Why do you speak of equality? Because when you speak of equality, it is that one is inferior; mostly, it is women who hold such views, because they always think that they are at the bottom end of the scale. Yet if you are at the bottom, you will remain at the bottom. Man and woman are created equal, and life itself imposes certain things upon the family. (Catholic priest 2)

Well, I speak as a priest! The man and the woman are equal, because both have received baptism in the Church, and both are children of God. Now, when people want to speak of equality, you see that we are in the domain of marriage, where they are not equal. There is a differentiated equality, which means that they are equal but different. Each has his or her level: it is the man who will demand the woman's hand in marriage, it is the man who pays the dowry, it is he who is the boss. Within the home, the woman cannot wear the pants (*porter le pantalon*). Unfortunately, the law encourages everyone to misunderstand equality, leading to an increase of divorces. (Catholic priest 3)

One of the interviewed priests warned against what he sees as a westernization of Africa in an amoral sense. He also denounced the very political and undemocratic character of the marriage reforms and expressed his belief that, like many other legal texts, these new laws will not be applied:

This law is truly modeled on the Westerners, so we must be very careful. There is a co-responsibility of the man and that woman, which is not a problem. If you will allow me to be a critic, it is that in Côte d'Ivoire we have more texts than laws. These texts are to adorn the archives; that's my view. We are witnessing a westernization of African societies, and they want us all to be on the same level. (Catholic priest 1)

The imams agreed with the Catholic priests in their reaffirmation of the religious foundation of marriage and in their critical view of the revision of the family code in Côte d'Ivoire. The only major difference between the two categories of religious leaders concerned the interpretation of the concept of equality. The two groups of religious leaders agreed that the superiority of man in the family does not mean that the man must dominate or mistreat his wife:

> What I am not ready to accept is that we say that the woman and the man are equal. Even the word "equal" is not good, because they don't have the same education. The word "equal" makes it so that today when you go before the courts, there are lots of problems there. We must not even employ the word "equal" between the man and the woman. (Imam 1)

> Islam says that men are superior to women, which means that men must take into account all the needs of women. Her health, her dress, her lodging, everything! But if, on the contrary, the man does not have the means, we will see how we can manage that. But to say that they are equal, the word is too big, and Islam is not here to support that. (Imam 2)

> The woman must submit to her husband, which does not mean that she is a slave to her husband. The two are not the same. When she submits herself with all her values, that also permits the man to lower himself. He says to himself, "She puts herself at my disposition, meaning that I must make her happy." But if the two are equal, meaning that the woman must do nothing in the home so that it is the servant who does everything—the woman must not touch anything because both men and women are in charge—you will see that the children who see that, will copy a behavior more serious than the parents, in saying that "I did not see my mother do this, I did not see my mother do that." (Imam 3)

> Equality, what does that mean? We consider the household, and because the woman works, we will share the electricity bill, we will share the children's schooling. We will share the food. And

religion says that it is you who are the leader. Why does the child take the father's name? It is because of this responsibility that he has, because of the power that he has in the home. The woman's dress is paid for by the man, he pays for the care of the children. It is such that all his power stems from these responsibilities. And Allah has said that the child who is born in his house will bear his name. (Imam 4)

In the imams' view, as in the view of married Muslim men, the man's financial responsibility for his family is the main foundation of his authority in the household.

State actors: A legislator and a magistrate. This section on men's perspectives will conclude with the interviews of two state actors, one a legislator and the other a magistrate.

The legislator, who is also first deputy mayor of one of the municipalities of the city of Abidjan, described the content of the family law reform in these terms: "It is a reform concerning several articles that have been deemed discriminatory. The reform simply says that the life of the couple must be balanced. It levels a certain number of things in the household. It is a law that has been poorly explained to the population, but it is not bad." He seemed to approve of all the reforms but would have liked "the proposal of polygamy instead of monogamy." What must above all be avoided, he said, is "to adopt an article on what you call homosexuality." He explained: "That is a phenomenon we must stamp out with great energy. If that comes, I will vote against it." Invited to elucidate his understanding of what equality between man and woman means, the legislator affirmed: "We do not speak of gender equality nor of income. It is within human rights that we speak of equality. Religion gives guidelines and instructs couples to form a single entity. Even local customs regulate marital relations. We know the duties of the man and those of the woman." The legislator's reference to religious and cultural traditions is notable; he relies on contextual factors to understand the meaning of the revised family code's provisions on equality.

The legislator favored complementarity as a way of understanding men's and women's roles in the household: "For me, there is not a specific role dedicated to a man or to a woman. They are complementary. It is there in customs as in religion. Regarding the law, it attempts to level the situation, which is to say, the gap between men and women." In his opinion, "The head of the family is naturally established in traditional and modern society; it is the man. The law attempts to level this, to avoid abuse and discrimination within the couple."

As for the magistrate, he summarized the content of the new provisions of the family code in these terms: "I know that at the level of reciprocal obligations that weigh on the man and the woman, there is an element that has left. There is no longer the notion of a head of the family. The two members of the couple proportionally manage the family's expenses." When asked for his opinion on the significance of this revision, the magistrate estimated that the law is not complete: "We must complete it, because if we have changed the obligation of the head of the family, there were certain obligations that weighed in an exclusive manner on the man before, which now must also be changed in these texts." But the magistrate declined to speak on the merits of the revision, invoking the nature of his position: "I abstain from responding to that question, because I am a magistrate. I must not bring judgment upon the legislator. I must apply the law."

Regarding the effective equality of the man and the woman, however, he clarified that there is a gap between law and reality: "The law is a set of ideas from the mind of a modern legislator, a "white" civilizer. But in practice, the behavior at home is such that man is head of the family. In other words, they made the law, but in practice it is not applied." Concerning the roles of the man and the woman in the home, the magistrate expressed preference for the complementary approach:

Each has his or her primordial role, as defined in the obligations that weigh on him or her to maintain the community of life. The man ensures survival of the family, and the woman is his helper. According to the Catholic church, the man is the head of the family. He has a moral obligation to ensure the well-being of the family. The Church says that woman must submit to her husband. It is the same for local customs.

Regarding the role of the head of the family, the magistrate made a distinction: "In my opinion, it is the man who is head of the family. According to the law, both the man and the woman are the head of the family. And according to custom and religion, the man is head of the family." Like numerous other stakeholders, the magistrate made the distinction between different spheres of application of the notion of equality.

CONCLUSION: EQUALITY AS DIFFERENTIATED COMPLEMENTARITY

Overall, Ivorian perspectives on modernity are marked by ambivalence: Ivorians appreciate having more freedom of choice and enjoying the benefits of technological and scientific advances, but when it comes to issues of sexuality and marriage, they are concerned about what they perceive as moral decline epitomized by the reference to homosexuality and same-sex marriage. In this light, gender reforms are looked upon with suspicion, as a plot by the West to corrupt African morals. Ivorians confess their ignorance of the details of the family code revision, but are sensitive to the aspects of the new law that most directly challenge their views on marriage and women's equality. The interviews feature differentiated notions of what equality means in the customary, secular, and religious spheres. A formal understanding of gender equality is confined to the secular sphere, but in both customary and religious spheres, gender equality is understood as the complementarity of the man and the woman, perceived as equal in dignity yet different.

Interviewees did not express opposition to the idea that the man remains head of the family. On the contrary, they argued that interpreting gender equality in terms of sharing the role of family head puts familial stability at risk. In a broader sense, they understood the notion of gender equality in several different ways and believed that it operates differently according to the context. The empirical data examined in this chapter demonstrated that many Ivorian men and women have a differentiated interpretation of equality based on a situational approach. The interviewees seem to adapt their positions to the demands of each social context. In this understanding, the meaning of equality depends on whether it is understood in a professional, religious, traditional, or legal environment.

Among Catholics and Muslims, the young and the old, men and women, the interviews and focus groups did not reveal major divergences on the question of who is the head of the family: they all agreed that it is the man. This unanimity is probably the product of shared processes of religious and cultural socialization. The new law in this case counteracts the dominant culture and seeks to change it.

Religion has been described as one of the major political forces of our time, and it certainly has undeniable power as a force in modern Africa, where spiritual practice has been shaped by a long and rich history. African epistemologies pervade power systems and impact communities, shaping a view of religion in which spiritual power is real and effective (Ellis and Ter Haar 1998 and 2007). Religion is inextricably linked to politics in a constant interplay of power relations. The connection between religion and political power is rooted in history, as in many precolonial societies power stemmed from the ability to uphold the cosmic order, with the result that authority lay with ritual experts and religious leaders (Ellis and Ter Haar 1998, 188). Thus, African epistemologies, in which religion holds a central place, operate at every level of society and shape popular understandings of social realities, including gender relations. Linda Woodhead explains, "Attention to gender demands attention to power because gender is inseparably bound up with the unequal distribution of power in society," and furthermore, "Religion's constitutive contribution to power relations within society is best understood by viewing religion itself as a system of power" (2013, 60–61). Cedric Mayson has pointed out that "Equality means transformation as well as participation" (2004, 53).

Modern Africa is certainly being transformed by the participation of religious leaders, organizations, and governments in efforts to balance progress against tradition. While much of the world has sought to develop by becoming increasingly secular, many African nations continue to take religious factors seriously in policy making. Traditions of religiosity shape understandings of the family in either positive or negative ways. Religion and politics in modern West Africa remain deeply connected realms of power.

CHAPTER FOUR

Regional and Comparative Perspectives

Senegal, Mali, and Niger

The three countries under consideration in this chapter are Senegal, Mali, and Niger, all of which are located in the Sahel region. The Sahel is a vast, semiarid zone of Africa located between the Sahara desert to the north and the tropical savannas to the south. It is the site of encounters between predominantly Islamic and nomadic northern cultures and southern Christian and traditional cultures. In Senegal, Niger, Mali, and Côte d'Ivoire, Islam is the religion of the majority of the population. Côte d'Ivoire shares borders with Senegal and Mali, and all four are former French colonies and members of the West African Economic and Monetary Union.

In most Sahel countries during the colonial period, the French administration did not abolish customary law. Instead, it was allowed to coexist with the newly introduced French law, and people had a choice between the two to regulate their family affairs. In general, as Dorothea Schulz explains, "French positive law was applied for the colonized population in urban areas, the *assimilés*, in other words, the new political elites and those who were French citizens," while "[l]ocally diverse customary laws regulated the rest of the population" (2003, 138). Indeed, Mali, Niger, and Senegal all emerged from a century of French colonization with a pluralist legal system that included a combination of customary law, Islamic law, and French civil law. Boye, Hill, Isaacs, and Gordis provide a useful overview of what happened next:

Since independence in 1960, Burkina Faso, Mali, and Senegal have each replaced the colonial family law they inherited from the French with national marriage codes. Mali enacted a Code of Marriage and Guardianship in 1962; Senegal enacted a family code in 1972; and Burkina Faso enacted a Code of Family and Persons in 1989. These post-independence marriage codes have in general integrated customary law and French colonial law into a more comprehensive family code in which all marriages—polygamous or monogamous—have civil legal status. Even though an ad hoc committee was created in 1976 to develop a family code, Niger has not yet formally adopted one. Consequently, marriages in Niger typically have either customary or civil status. (1991, 344–45)

In all of these countries, there is also a rural-urban disparity in how family law is applied. They are predominantly rural, and "in rural areas, most Sahelian marriages are still governed by customary law" (346). Gender reforms considered in this book, by contrast, are urban processes that do not significantly include rural voices.

This chapter provides an overview of the social forces involved in the politics surrounding family codes reforms in Senegal, Niger, and Mali. In each of these countries, women's organizations have been at the forefront of gender reforms. In Senegal, the state remains the main initiator of gender reforms but has consistently privileged a consensus approach while containing the resistance of conservative religious forces. Niger has no official family code adopted by the state. So far, post-independence attempts to establish one have failed due to resistance mounted by Islamic organizations. In Mali, a new family law was adopted in 2011 after almost thirteen years of wide-ranging consultations. But toward the end of the process, Islamic organizations stepped up the pressure on the state and succeeded in having the final version tailored to their wishes, to the dismay of more progressive forces. Overall, although religious organizations are the most vocal conservative forces in these countries, each country has its own power dynamics surrounding the politics of gender reforms. Attempts to reform the family code in the three countries have been fraught with tensions and conflicts between the secular state, the religious authorities, and the traditional authorities. This might explain why the secular state in

Côte d'Ivoire chose to bypass religious organizations during the reform of its family code.

SENEGAL AND THE CONTAINMENT OF
CONSERVATIVE FORCES

Senegal is undoubtedly one of the most stable democratic countries in West Africa, with a notable tradition of religious tolerance characterized by respect for religious minorities. Senegal has a population of 13.5 million, of which 49.9 percent are men and 50.1 percent are women (Agence Nationale de la Statistique et de la Démographie, 2014). The majority of the population, about 54.8 percent, lives in rural areas. According to Pew Research Center (2015) estimates, the Senegalese population is about 96 percent Muslim, 3.5 percent Christian, and 0.5 percent other religions. Fatou Sarr (2019) has argued that in Sufi Islam, which is dominant in Senegal, it would be misleading to describe gender relationships in terms of the oppression of women by men. In the history of Muslim brotherhoods in Senegal, women have played significant roles, and the most prominent of these women still hold a central place in the collective consciousness of the brotherhoods.[1] Sarr explains that it would be equally misleading to assess the situation of Muslim women in Senegal through the lens of recent religious ideologies, such as Salafism, imported from some Arab countries.

Sufi influence is a driving force in Senegalese cultural life and exerts its influence on a variety of social practices (Augis 2012, 432). Although religious leaders influence public life in ways that have a significant impact on women, the dynamism of women's organizations in Senegal also enhances women's participation in societal debates and struggles (Kane 2008; N'Diaye 2016). Catherine Marshall has underscored the vitality of women's organizations and their activism in favor of women's rights in both religious and secular circles; she also points out that such organizations contend with tensions surrounding "secular principles and approaches, in large measure around the roles of religious beliefs and, above all, religious actors in contemporary politics and social policies." She holds that "Nowhere has this been more significant than with respect to women's rights and roles" (2017, 141).

Political authorities have in general refrained from confronting religious authorities who command public respect, fearing social upheaval and negative electoral consequences.

These tensions between government reform and religious authority have roots going back to the immediate postcolonial period. In 1960, Senegal achieved independence from France. The following year, a commission was set up by the then head of state, Léopold Sédar Senghor, to make an inventory of local customs on the regulation of family life. The results revealed a great diversity of practices.[2] In 1965, President Senghor set up a thirty-two-member commission to work on the family code. This commission included parliamentarians, magistrates, Muslim judges, and representatives of customary and religious authorities. Its mission was to carefully examine all the data gathered by the previous commission. Its conclusions helped feed the reflections of the drafting committee of the family code, set up in July 1966 and entrusted with the responsibility of harmonizing the various types of family law. This was a consensus-building project that attempted a synthesis of traditional law derived from local customs, Islamic law emanating from the Quran, and modern law inspired by the French legal system (Brossier 2004, 80). The result was the family code adopted as Law No. 72–61 of June 12, 1972. Its main characteristics included the harmonization of the law, the affirmation of the secular character of society, the recognition of the principle of individual rights, and the equality of all citizens.

During the process, a number of Muslim religious leaders gathered under the umbrella of the Conseil Supérieur Islamique and wrote to then prime minister Abdou Diouf to voice their opposition to some of the provisions of the draft family code that they believed contradicted the Islamic faith. Their concerns were ignored. Religious leaders did not insist, partly because of internal disagreements; instead, they bowed to the 1972 family code adopted by the National Assembly. However, the new family code was diversely received across the nation. The spiritual leader of the Mourides[3] in particular challenged its enforcement in the city of Touba   as would happen again in 2010.

Following the Nairobi World Conference on Women in 1985, the rise of women's rights organizations in Senegal strengthened women's resistance to religious fundamentalists' attempts to reverse the evolution of the family code. This struggle, spearheaded mainly by women, led to the adoption in 1989 of Law No. 89–01, which amended the 1972 family code. The revision improved the status of women in marriage by reducing the husband's power and control over his wife. Revisions allowed women to provisionally administer the property of an absent husband, to possess their own copy of the marriage certificate, to practice the profession of their choice, and to have a say in the choice of the location of the family residence. Following this modification, women's rights organizations made additional attempts to lobby for the limitation of polygamy to two wives, but due to the resistance mounted by some religious leaders, this initiative failed. In the meantime, the religious landscape of Senegal had begun to shift. Wahhabi religious ideologies were introduced in Senegal in the 1970s. The Wahhabi wanted to reform the version of Islam practiced by the Muslim brotherhoods. They established their legitimacy by investing in social programs, especially in the 1980s, when structural adjustment programs weakened the ability of the state to provide social services. Islamist organizations, through many NGOs, provided valuable support for education, health, and access to water and to food.

In 1996, Sheikh Abdoulaye Dieye, a religiously conservative politician, founded a religious political party, and the family code became a target of his fierce critiques. He attempted to push back the family law reforms with the creation in 1996 of the Committee for the Reform of the Family Code in Senegal (CIRCOFS) by the Conseil Supérieur Islamique. This council was founded in 1974 to advocate for the application of Shari'a in Senegal (Mbow 2010). CIRCOFS favored the creation of an Islamic State in Senegal, the restoration of the father's ability to repudiate illegitimate children and deprive them of their rights, and the maintenance of the father's authority in the family. Under the leadership of barrister Babacar Niang, CIRCOFS held a conference in Dakar on October 12, 2002, to present a draft code that would replace the 1972 family code (CIRCOFS 2002). However, the then head of the state, Abdoulaye Wade, did not endorse the initiative. CIRCOFS refused to back down, launching a nationwide sensitization campaign that led to building multiple alliances with other religious groups. Imam Mbaye Niang, leader of a pro-Islamist party supporting the CIRCOFS initiative, said: "If Wade does not change his mind, he will be punished at the time of the elections. . . . The caliphs [marabouts] have all signed our text for the reform" (Lamlili 2003).

But not all Senegalese were in favor of this reform, and scores of NGOs, MPs, academics, and intellectuals denounced the reform project as a blow to women's rights. A feminist platform called Siggil Jigeen, made up of eighteen associations, spearheaded resistance to the CIRCOFS project. According to Siggil Jigeen's president, Safietou Diop, this project constituted a danger to national cohesion: "The Senegalese are very peaceful and live in harmony under the current code," she declared (quoted in Lamlili 2003). According to Diop, the members of CIRCOFS were misusing religion to serve their own political interests: "They are misreading the Qur'an, only to serve their interests" (quoted in Lamlili 2003). Overall, the pressure from religious leaders to reverse the previous reforms failed to translate into a new code, indicating that the revival religious movements, in spite of their growing influence, had not yet secured enough support, especially among the leaders of the religious brotherhoods, to achieve their aims.

In 1999, Senegal modified its penal code to pass Law No. 99–05 banning all forms of violence against women. A second bill on the reform of parental authority was not adopted, however. According to Fatou Sarr (2019), the family code has made remarkable progress since the independence of Senegal—except on issues of polygamy and divorce.

In 2004, the Association for the Defense of Secularism and National Unity in Senegal was formed. It brought together various networks and platforms that agreed on the need for joint mobilization to preserve national unity, secularism, and democratic achievements. To counter the demands of the Islamic committee, the organization launched its own campaign and worked to delegitimize and discredit CIRCOFS. Beginning in 2007, women's organizations launched a battle for the Parity Act, which, although initially rejected by the Constitutional Council, was finally adopted in 2010. The passage of the Parity Act led to violent reactions from extremist political and religious actors, who described it as a Masonic law. The leaders of religious brotherhoods did not critique the reform, however, because the head of state had worked in advance to secure their approval. But the application of the law in Touba, the religious headquarters of the Mourides, proved to be a difficult undertaking. Sarr notes that "Mouride authorities have rejected national legislation requiring specific percentages of women on electoral lists, and the government has tacitly accepted the position" (2019, 115). The fact that a religious leader can rule against the application of a state law in his area of influence is indicative of some of the power dynamics in Senegal (Camara 2007; Mbow 2010).

The context of Senegal is one of growing public influence of fundamentalist religious groups with conservative agendas intended to reverse some of the progress the state has made on women's rights. The competition between these religious groups for social influence in Senegal mirrors the rivalries between the Middle Eastern powers that sponsor them to advance their religious ideologies locally. These fundamentalist religious movements paint secularism as a Western import inimical to religious values and they are the single greatest threat to the secular state in Senegal. Their strategies for political and social influence and control include alliances to fight against secularism, freemasonry, and homosexuality; the founding of religious political parties; humanitarian and social intervention among the poorest sections of the population; religious teachings; and extensive use of mass media. In response, Sufis and reformists tend to put aside their own religious rivalries to form a united front when it comes to resisting gender reforms.

The informal alliance between the state and women's organizations in support of gender reforms is noteworthy. It remains to be seen if radical religious groups will succeed in securing the support they need among the populace to defeat secular forces through democratic processes. So far, in spite of the alliance between the Sufi and the reformists—the two main versions of Islam in Senegal—in opposition to the reforms made to the family code since 1972, Muslim leaders have not been able to halt or reverse the progress made on women's rights. According to Marième N'Diaye, this is because Sufi Islam, which is still practiced by the majority of Senegalese, has a long history of a privileged relationship with the state, which has preserved its social influence. These privileges are still more important to the leaders of the brotherhoods than their alliances with the reformists to oppose state-initiated gender reforms. In other words, "The fragmentation of the Islamic camp helps us to understand why it has failed to prevent substantial reforms towards greater gender equality in the family, despite its weight both politically and socially" (2016, 73).

NIGER AND THE POWER OF CONSERVATIVE FORCES

Gender roles have evolved in Niger over the centuries, beginning with the arrival of Islam in the eighth century (see Dunbar 1991; Diakité 2016). According to Ousseina Alidou (2005), competing pulls to modernize under Western and Islamic influence have prescribed different gender roles with distinct experiences for Muslim men and women. For some ethnic groups, such as the Tuareg and Fulani, conversion to Islam promoted new practices of polygyny and sedentarization, altering gender relations. European colonization also promoted a new gender ideology, which privileged Muslim men in the labor field.

While the Islamic-influenced norms enforced in contemporary Niger tend to exclude women from public power politics and define masculinity in strict terms, female-run organizations created to promote Islam, as well as economic opportunities, have also led to female solidarity and empowerment. Over time, power negotiations realigned gender relations so that conceptions of the roles of Nigerien women and men blended old and new meanings. French colonialism, development agendas in the 1960s, structural adjustment programs in the 1980s, and democratization in the 1990s all modernized Niger in their own ways and affected the status of women, as did the rise of political Islam. Yet as the relationship between religion and gender in Niger continues to change, modernity opens new spaces for reforms. Many Muslim women now use Islam to create an alternative reality with room for them in public and civic life, developing an agenda to advocate for increased equality (Alidou 2005, 188–89). On May 13, 1991, for example, about twenty thousand women marched against women's underrepresentation in the preparatory committee for the National Conference.

The attitude of Nigerien officials toward religion is ambivalent. According to its constitution and its French-inspired policy of *laïcité*, or secularism, Niger is a secular state, yet in reality the line between state and religious power is blurred. In the framework of *laïcité*, emphasized particularly since the period of democratization in the 1990s, the state has resisted the influence of organized Islam on state politics (Sounaye 2009). Democratization is seen as providing an opportunity to develop a state free from the French colonizers, military rule, and religious influence. Yet Islam has never left the public domain in Niger.

In seeking to legitimize their authority, state officials and politicians turn to religion. Many social groups in Niger are either explicitly Islamic or founded on Islamic principles, and groups of both types influence political and economic realities, pushing back against a secular policy that is not understood to represent the majority of Nigeriens' wishes.

French colonial rule in Niger laid the foundation for a complex legal system, which has had a lasting impact on the current state. Family law is very much influenced by customary and religious law, as the state has recourse to both traditional and religious authorities in official courts to rule on family-related incidents. Judges must "apply the customs of the parties," and if the parties are Muslim, "the customs" refers to Islamic law (Kang 2015, 29). State judges who are not trained in religious law consult Islamic experts to interpret and adjudicate in cases of family disputes; this practice began under French colonial officials, who assumed that customary family law in Niger was Islamic. The courts separated "citizens" from "subjects" by applying either French Napoleonic codes or customary Islamic law depending on whether one was a European or an African. The Nigerien chiefs and religious leaders who held legal power at this time were almost exclusively male, so family law was shaped without women's input, and it continues to reflect this initial gender imbalance (Kang 2015, 41–42). Niger's 1960 constitution proclaimed Niger to be a "secular, democratic, and social Republic" but maintained the French colonial policy of preserving Islamic law as a local custom. The contradictory nature of this state, which is purportedly secular yet utilizes religious law to settle family matters, has affected gender equality and community justice.

To date, Niger has no official family code, as previous attempts to adopt one have failed due to the resistance mounted against it by Islamic associations. Modern scholars debate whether secularism or religiosity is more beneficial to women in Niger. Both approaches are influenced by the patriarchal legacies of family law that favors men (Alidou and Alidou 2008, 27). Efforts to reform the family code have sought to promote gender equality in Niger; Barbara Cooper writes that such attempts provoke "an immediate firestorm of outrage from traditionalist and reformist leaders alike," and "[t]he popular base upon which such reforms can be built is quite difficult to mobilize" (2010,

104). As a result, the state has repeatedly given in to the pressure of Niger's religious constituencies.

Nigerien women have been at the forefront of the struggle for a family code that can protect them from abuses, particularly those related to repudiation and inheritance. In the 1960s, through the association Union des Femmes du Niger (UFN), which was affiliated with the ruling party (the African Democratic Rally party), women asked for new legislation on marriage that would give mothers of four children "legal protection against repudiation" (Clair 1965, 178). Their demand was not granted. In 1975, under General Seyni Kountché's regime, the idea of drafting a family code was finally accepted by the government. That same year, the Association des Femmes du Niger (AFN) was founded and listed the adoption of a family code as one of its priorities. It then set up a special commission to carry out a study of the customs and traditions of the various cultural communities in Niger and to sensitize women to the idea and importance of a family code.

But the Association des Femmes du Niger's family code project did not please the Islamic Association of Niger, which had been created in 1974 to represent and defend the interests of Islam in the country. The idea of the family code was therefore set aside until 1985, when it was relaunched at a seminar organized by the AFN in collaboration with the Ministry of Health. Harassed by inheritance disputes, General Kountché instructed the minister of justice to establish a family code committee, which was set up in January 1987. The democratization process in the 1990s resulted in the blossoming of women's and Islamic associations scrambling for the control of public space. Two more women's organizations, the Democratic Rally of Nigerien Women and the Association of Female Jurists of Niger, took up the cause of the family code and made it a public issue. Major Islamic associations radicalized their opposition to the project, however, when a draft code was made public in January 1993. In 1998, another problem arose around the CEDAW, whose ratification was blocked by the same Islamic associations (Alio 2005).

In this struggle for gender reforms, political parties have handled the question with prudence to avoid offending the electorate in a country where Muslims represent 98.7 percent of the population. After the failure of the 1993 attempt, the promoters of the code and the Ministry for Women's Advancement decided to change their strategy. Women's rights activists rallied again in the early 2000s (Kang 2015), and on June 7, 2000, the National Assembly adopted Law No. 2000–008 on quotas, which stipulates that for elected offices, at least one-tenth of the elected representatives in each party must be women, and 25 percent or more of political appointees should be women. This measure significantly raised the level of representation of women in bodies like the National Assembly, which had a single woman representative among the 83 parliamentarians of the first Assembly of the Fifth Republic (1999–2004), compared to 27 women of 171 parliamentarians in 2017. The law adopted in 2002 was revised by Law No. 2014–64 of November 5, 2014, which raised the quota for women serving elective functions to 15 percent from 10 percent.[4] Such reforms were immediately beneficial to women, but mainly to educated and urban women, as rural and poor women were often not able to participate in these processes. Not all women support the reforms, moreover; the dividing line among women is often framed in terms of the secularist woman versus the Islamist woman (Alidou and Alidou 2008; Cooper 2010).

Beginning in 2002, the Ministry for Women's Advancement secured from the World Bank a grant for the Institutional Development Fund for the Improvement of Women's Legal Status. The grant was used to conduct a study on the legal status of women in Niger. That study revealed the persistence of discriminatory norms against women, the existence of nondiscriminatory standards that were not enforced, and legal gaps that needed to be filled. Reviewed by thirty traditional and thirty regional leaders and validated in 2003, the study was used by the Ministry for Women's Advancement to elaborate, with the support of the African Development Bank, a project entitled Strengthening Gender Equity. The old idea of a family code was thus abandoned in favor of a more general notion of a personal status code, and the quest for consensus was also set aside right from the beginning of the process. Instead, the Ministry for Women's Advancement developed programs and strategies for women's economic empowerment, help with household chores, and the political advancement of women (Alio 2005).

Central to the new strategy to promote women's rights was securing the support of influential religious leaders and movements. Specific programs and projects that resulted from this strategy include the development in July 2008 of a comprehensive national gender policy through the Ministry for the Advancement of Women and Child Protection, the development of training modules on Islam and gender-based violence for religious leaders, the adoption in 2003 of a law punishing practitioners of female genital mutilation, the adoption in 2006 of a law on reproductive health allowing women to access modern contraception without their husbands' authorization, and the adoption in 2008 of the National Gender Policy to correct gender inequities and inequalities and implement the constitutional principles of equality and nondiscrimination. Newfound efforts through the Ministry of Justice began in 2010 when a Nigerien consultancy group wrote a draft of a family law. The group drafted a new family law and sought feedback from various Muslim and Christian groups.

Despite efforts to get the draft accepted, the bill was criticized by scores of Islamic groups that described it as satanic and against Islam; Muslim leaders depicted it as a feminist text that would disrupt sacred family values (Kang 2015, 72–73; Cooper 2010). In the Nigerien context, where the small non-Muslim Christian minority tends to identify with French civil law over Muslim law, Nigeriens on the whole associate civil law with Christianity. Thus, religious leaders often see attempts to institute a family code as "un-Islamic Western intrusions"; Niger's political culture "has long been implicitly or explicitly Islamic" (Cooper 2010).

The case of Niger shows how, in spite of the failure of the family code project, the state, with the support of numerous partners, has nonetheless made a notable effort to promote women's rights. The activism and resilience of women's organizations in such difficult circumstances is also noteworthy. But even more notable is the state's change of strategy in the face of religious opposition. Instead of taking a comprehensive approach to gender reforms, state officials have settled on a piecemeal approach that seeks to implement gender equality first in areas most likely to gain the support of religious leaders, such as political representation, health care, and education. The state has initiated several projects and programs for women's empowerment, training, and strategies for reaching a consensus in future actions that are likely to upset the sensitivity of religious groups or customary circles.

MALI AND A TAILORED FAMILY CODE

Mali has 14.5 million inhabitants, of which 50.4 percent are women and 70 percent are rural dwellers. About 95 percent of the population is Muslim, and the remaining 5 percent is made up of Christians and members of traditional religions (Institut National de la Statistique du Mali 2015). In spite of its overwhelmingly Muslim population, Mali has been a constitutionally secular country since its independence in 1960. But, as the politics of the family code in Mali show, while Islam is not a state religion, it plays a central role in the lives of Malians and influences the way public affairs are run. Although Mali boasts a long tradition of religious tolerance, its stability is threatened today by jihadist groups operating from the northern part of the country.

Islam in Mali is ancient, dating to the ninth century, and has evolved to have many faces as a result of historical, political, religious, and economic processes (Brenner 1993; Pellerin and Trotignon 2010; Soares 2005). The main divide today is between traditional Sufi brotherhoods, credited with a long tradition of tolerance, and the reformist Sunni Wahhabis, who are less tolerant of other forms of religious expression. Wahhabism entered Mali in the 1970s. During the dictatorial rule of Moussa Traoré, the Wahhabis gained some influence by instrumentalizing their links to Saudi Arabia and the Islamic Development Bank, both of which gave them bargaining power. These links allowed the Malian state to access about $600 million in foreign aid between 1970 and 1980 (Holder 2013, 152). Following the democratic revolution of 1991, the Wahhabis were politically weakened by the trend toward liberalization, which led to the growth of private initiatives and the rise of new Islamic organizations. But the Wahhabis found new, fertile ground in the social sector, where they developed networks of educational institutions, units of reflection, charitable associations, and a strong presence in the media. They preach virulently against the Islam of local Sufi brotherhoods, calling for reform of Sufi beliefs and practices (Otayek 1993). This divergence of ideologies within the same religion is not specific to Islam; Christianity has its own share of sectarian rivalries in Mali.

Mali became independent in 1960 with a constitution that granted equal civil and political rights to women, but this equality did not translate into its first family code (Code du Mariage et de la Tutelle), which was adopted in 1962. According to Dorothea Schulz, "Strategies of evasion and of passive resistance added to the state's inability to enforce the new legal regulations in the rural hinterlands and rendered much of the legislation obsolete" (2003, 141). In 1991, in Mali as in many other countries in sub-Saharan Africa, a wind of democratization was blowing, and popular uprisings led to the fall of the dictatorial regime of Moussa Traoré. This change aroused great hope for political liberalization among the populace, especially among women and youth. Malian women seized the opportunity and set up multiple associations and other nongovernmental organizations to defend their rights. Thus, the new constitution adopted in 1991 stipulated in its preamble that the Republic of Mali would defend the rights of women and children. The constitution also upheld the principle of equality and prohibited discrimination based on sex.

The Association of Malian Jurists initiated debate on the best ways and means of assisting political authorities to implement a constitutional commitment to women's rights. A group was set up to draft a document proposing special legal provisions for the improvement of the status of women as citizens, wives, and mothers in the democracy. A Legal Reform Support Group made up of experts in the different fields of law was established by the Malian Female Lawyers' Association. This group reviewed various existing texts to identify forms of discrimination that affected Malian women, especially in the light of all the international conventions for the protection and promotion of women's rights already ratified by Mali. The end result was a document entitled "The Situation of Women in Malian Positive Law and Its Prospects for Development," which acknowledged the progress made in adapting the domestic legal system to the standards of the international community but also expressed a need for improvement to better take into account the principle of equality. It suggested that a National Observatory on Women's Rights be created to work in conjunction with the Office for the Advancement of Women in taking up the agenda of gender equality.

The coordinator of the Office for the Advancement of Women undertook to endorse the recommendations of the study and to consider their implementation a priority for the government. The office was re-named the Ministry for the Promotion of Women, Children, and the Family. One of the priorities of the ministry was to review all domestic legal texts to identify areas of discrimination and fill legal gaps where necessary. To this end, the ministry set up an interministerial commis-sion, enlarged to include members of civil society, to conduct a study of texts related to the family code. The reflection and review process began in 1998 and lasted more than ten years. The proposal to reform the Code du Mariage et de la Tutelle was part of a larger project enti-tled Promotion de la Démocratie et de la Justice au Mali, which was generously funded by Western donors and supported by women's orga-nizations and the Ministry for the Promotion of Women, Children, and the Family. After a long period of nationwide consultations, the first draft of the Code of Persons and the Family was adopted by the government during the Council of Ministers meeting on May 13, 2009. It was then submitted to the National Assembly, which voted in its favor on August 3, 2009, by a large majority. The code was understood to be highly consensual and innovative. It was the result of wide-ranging consultations that involved most religious, political, economic, and social factions in Mali. It introduced important innovations in areas such as inheritance, marriage, kinship, filiation, nationality, di-vorce, and marital regimes.

Despite the code's popular reception by many in Malian society, some Islamic groups were critical of it. The most forceful opposition was mounted by a national association of Muslims (Association Ma-lienne pour l'Unité et le Progrès de l'Islam, AMUPI). It should be noted that on the issue of opposing the family code, Muslims in Mali managed to put aside their internal doctrinal quarrels to form a united front. Members of the National Muslim Women Association of Mali, known as L'Union Nationale des Associations des Femmes Musul-manes du Mali, chose to side with AMUPI to oppose the reform in-stead of supporting women activists. This alignment might have had something to do with the class divide among women, reflecting the im-portance of the rural-urban divide in women's experiences and view-points over the male-female divide (Schulz 2003, 158).

A meeting of more than fifty thousand people was organized by Muslim leaders in the largest stadium in the capital city of Bamako.[5] To oppose the code, several religious leaders had made the trip to Bamako from remote regions. Meetings were held in a number of other major cities in Mali as well. Faced with this front of religious protest, the public authorities, political parties, and civil society—with a few rare exceptions—kept a low profile and ultimately retreated. They had underestimated the reaction of the religious leaders. To contain the growing movement, which had begun to convey messages to an agitated populace that were unrelated to the adoption of the code, the head of state, after consulting several stakeholders, made an address to the nation and referred the code back to the National Assembly for re-examination.

Muslim organizations issued a document detailing their concerns about the adopted version of the family code, which they argued did not take into account Malian religious and societal realities. These included, among other things, the description of marriage as a secular act, the fixing of the minimum marriage age at eighteen years for women, the provision of divorce on the basis of the wife's refusal to contribute to household expenses, and the legitimation of children born out of wedlock. Regarding the definition of marriage as a secular act, the document reads: "To hold that there are no good grounds . . . for the attribution of legal effect to religious marriage is, on the one hand, to refuse to admit that in Mali, religious clerics do celebrate more marriages than the civil status registrars, and on the other hand, it means contempt for millions of Malian women married only under the rule of religion."[6] Benjamin Soares has argued that, during the process of the reform of the family code, "for many Malians, one of the most serious problems with the proposed reforms was that religious marriage would still not be legally recognized," because "the idea that a marriage conducted according to the rules of Islamic jurisprudence [could] be deemed illegitimate" was "deeply offensive" to many. He concludes that, "in the public discussions and debates about the reform of family law, the question of legal recognition of religious marriage was to become a major point of contention" (2009, 415).

Given that most Malians prefer religious marriage to civil marriage, what kind of accommodation can best serve the interests of the women meant to be empowered by the reform of the family code? The bottom line is that in spite of the existence of family codes, most marriages take place outside of the reach of state law, depriving most women of formal legal protection. The reluctance of the state to recognize religious marriages seems to imply that women are not better off in the hands of male clerics who are more inclined to uphold patriarchal values and structures. But the issue is the ability of the state to enforce its own family codes to ensure that the legal protection of women in marriage becomes a reality.

Ultimately, when the Malian family code was referred back to the National Assembly for further examination, a joint commission was created made up of members of the Haut Conseil Islamique and parliamentary legal experts. Following the work of that committee, a new draft of the code was presented to the National Assembly and adopted on December 2, 2011, which embodied the victory of the conservative agenda carried by the Haut Conseil Islamique. There was no strong, open protest against the new version of the code. At the time of its adoption, however, the minister of justice chose not to be at the National Assembly to present it to lawmakers. Written comments and letters of protest were sent to the minister of justice and the head of state. Nonetheless, the revised version prevailed, and the Haut Conseil Islamique got most of the changes they wanted.

The process of the adoption of the family code in Mali underscores the weight of Muslim organizations in public life and their influence over the state, which to preserve social peace had to renounce the progressive vision of the early version of the code. Taken as a whole, the process further highlights the hybrid nature of Mali, a country torn between the desire for modernity and its deep rootedness in tradition and religion. But Soares has cautioned against attributing the failure of the initial attempt to reform the family code in Mali solely to the increased influence of Islamism and religiously conservative Muslims. "The wide gap between Malian family-related civil law and the lived experiences and social practices of many Malians, who are overwhelmingly Muslim," he argues, "has become even more apparent in this era of political liberalization and promotion of global human rights discourses" (2009, 406). In spite of the existence of a family code established from the independence era in 1962, many couples in Mali, especially in rural areas, do not register their marriages with the state. As Soares put it, "For some Malians (Muslims and non-Muslims), not having a civil marriage has long been and remains a form of resistance to the state and its institutions. Moreover, many Malians live far from the government offices in which they are supposed to register" (406).

In Côte d'Ivoire, the secular state bypassed religious authorities and sped through a reform of the family code that enforces gender equality in an unprecedented way. In Mali, Senegal, and Niger, where Muslims constitute 90 percent of the population, these processes were slower and more inclusive of religious organizations, especially of conservative Muslim organizations and authorities. These authorities had the opportunity not only to voice their views but also to influence the reform. In Senegal, the secular state was more successful in containing the religious forces than in Mali and Niger. To date, Côte d'Ivoire is the only Muslim-majority country in Africa that, without provoking much social turmoil, has gone as far as removing from its family code the provision that man is the head of the family. One could argue that this was made possible by the fact that conservative religious forces have a very weak public voice and influence in Côte d'Ivoire, which is not the case in the other three countries where religious organizations have a powerful political influence.

In Senegal, Mali, and Niger, gender equality is a principle enshrined in their respective constitutions. The problem is that this principle has not yet been fully translated into family codes, which in many respects continue to discriminate against women, especially in relation to the choice of profession, processes of divorce or repudiation, custody of children in the event of a divorce, inheritance, choice of residence, and polygamy.

Religious leaders' resistance to the neoliberal framework of these reforms, which emphasize individual freedom and equality, is evident. Since colonization, the concept of the nuclear family and an individualistic understanding of human freedoms have gained ground in many African countries. But as Soares points out, "it is important to note that Malians generally think of marriage as the bringing together of kin groups, rather than simply an affair of individuals" (2009, 411). Although there is more freedom today in the choice of marriage partners in sub-Saharan Africa, many people still value the legitimation of the marriage by the community, as symbolized by customary rituals and the practice of bride wealth.

The processes of family law reform in the past six decades in Africa show that international pressure, political will, the generosity of foreign donors, and the vitality of local civil society organizations in general and of women's organizations in particular are instrumental in advancing the cause of women's rights and gender equality. The resistance of conservative religious groups and the weakness of states in enforcing progressive family laws remain major obstacles on the way to gender equality. In countries where the state's moral legitimacy or authority is in question, religious leaders tend to step in and reposition themselves as guardians of the traditional moral values of the community, portrayed as threatened by the corruption of secular Western forces. In such a context, the traditional interventionist (top-down) approach to social engineering is bound to fail.

The fragmentation of religion's authority, of the political landscape, and of civil society have all made it difficult for dogmatic and totalitarian interpretations of social life to prevail, introducing an opportunity for a more deliberative approach to societal reforms. Processes of gender reform involve the negotiation of power relationships between a variety of stakeholders, including international organizations, state actors, religious actors and groups, women's organizations, human rights organizations (civil society), and the population. But the most critical of all these stakeholders are conservative religious leaders, especially where they exert social influence at the grassroots level. Indeed, "[t]he capacity of civil society to produce contestation and democratic change becomes particularly constrained where religious actors and scripts gain a strong foothold in the political and social arenas" (Razavi and Jenichen 2010, 839–40). Patterns of gender reform are also shaped by countries' diverse historical and political trajectories. In general, however, political actors tend to bow to influential religious leaders to preserve their political capital. They avoid direct confrontation with influential religious leaders in order to avoid negative electoral consequences. Even in democratic contexts, politicians require allies to secure re-election, "and religious organizations are often good alliance partners as they are able to tap into a sizeable social network" (Razavi and Jenichen 2010, 842).

CHAPTER FIVE

The Hegemonic Entanglements of African Modernity

The study of gender politics undertaken in this book provides an opportunity to assess the many ways in which Africans receive, interpret, and reshape modernities. This chapter highlights some of the main traps of hegemonic modernities but also constructively looks at alternative ways of engaging them. A section on legal reform and social change considers the limitations of a prescriptive, legalistic approach to human rights in the West African context. We then develop an argument for a differentiated, democratic approach to gender reform that includes religion and avoids the hegemonic traps of an elitist process. This leads in the final section to a proposal for a more dialogical approach to gender reform that aims to reconcile African cultural and religious traditions with international norms by grounding universal notions of human rights in a community narrative for the sake of social legitimacy.

LEGAL REFORMS AND SOCIAL CHANGE

The subject of law has received a great deal of attention in anthropology, which points to the "intimate relation between law and society," in that "law is part of social life in general and must be treated analytically as such" (Moore 1969, 256; see also Conley and O'Barr 1993). The literature on legal anthropology addresses rules, judicial processes, litigation cases, legal institutions, and the law and social change, to name some examples. On the topic of law and social change, Sally Moore writes: "Many lawyers and law professors view law as an instrument for controlling society and directing social change, but most anthropologists are concerned with law as a reflection of a particular social order" (1969, 283). That is, is the law a prescriptive or a descriptive device? Given the often-noted difference between laws on the books and what is observed in practice, the prescriptive nature of law is evident. The gap between state law and observed practices is characteristic of the workings of family law in many African countries and points to a serious limitation of legal interventionism as a means for social change (Breton-Le Goff 2013). In every society, law operates as an instrument not only of social order but also of social change. But, as Moore pointed out, the tendency to understand the law as "an almost magical instrument of rapid reform" is "itself a ready-made field for investigation" (1969, 287). Inherent in any family law are ideas of what family is or should be. Family law reforms in the developing world have revealed the difficulty of applying foreign family law to a particular people without "a sort of ideological redesigning of the family" in that society (Anderson 1968; see also Freedman 1968).

In addition to investigating legal pluralism, recent legal anthropology has been interested in how "legal institutions and actors create meanings," as well as "the impact of these meanings on surrounding social relationships, and the effect of the cultural framework on the nature of legal procedures themselves" (Merry 1992, 360; see also Goodale 2017). Furthermore, there has been renewed attention to the relationship between law and power, including how law "constructs and deconstructs power relations" (Merry 1992, 360; see also Starr and Collier 1989). Particularly relevant for this debate is the anthropological interest in the impact of the transnationalization of human rights on local legal, political, and social processes (Goodale 2017, 3). In 2006, Sally Engle Merry, a pioneer in this area of research, wrote, "There has been little anthropological attention to the process by which universal human rights ideas are adopted and applied locally, particularly in areas other than indigenous rights" (40). One notable recent contribution to the anthropology of normative production is Gaëlle Breton-Le Goff's study of the translation of CEDAW into Congolese national law in order to address the problem of violence against women. Breton-Le

Goff showed how such processes of the production and implementation of new gender norms are necessarily constrained and sometimes distorted by the dominant customary cultural matrix and inherent collective values (2013).

In the past century, efforts around the world have sought to improve legal systems to promote equality and justice. In 1948, the Universal Declaration of Human Rights set out a list of inalienable rights for all people regardless of religion, race, or gender, creating a framework for bolstering all forms of equality under international law. Additions to the United Nations Charter in 1979 reaffirmed commitments to the equal dignity and worth of all. Moreover, UN members adopted a new international treaty, the Convention on the Elimination of All Forms of Discrimination against Women, that same year. The basic principles of CEDAW legally bind states to ensure women's rights and protect against discrimination, especially in areas of civil law such as property ownership and contract settlement, which traditionally favor men (Jeppie, Moosa, and Roberts 2010a, 46). Signatories to CEDAW include many African nations faced with the challenge of translating international law into their national legislation without irritating the guardians of local traditions and religious leaders or provoking social uprisings.

Following the Millennium Summit in 2000, most African countries committed themselves to achieving the Millennium Development Goals, one of which deals with gender equality and the empowerment of women (MDG 3). Consequently, gender integration through policy documents and development programs has become an imperative. This is why African states meeting in Maputo, Mozambique, in 2003 adopted a new protocol to the African Charter on Human and Peoples' Rights on the Rights of Women in Africa, referred to as the Maputo Protocol (Esimai 2007, 135). The Maputo Protocol seeks to address gender disparity through state legislation, detailing rights to inheritance, education, peace, food security, divorce, and more. It adheres to the tenets of CEDAW by focusing on provisions of family law and defining gender violence as causing physical, sexual, psychological, or economic harm that restricts fundamental freedoms in private or public life (137). This definition attempts to make gender equality relevant in discussions of international human rights law, signaling an African commitment to reform. The Maputo Protocol has been ratified by many states in Central and West Africa, including Senegal, Benin, and Cameroon, and has been signed by others, such as Niger and Côte d'Ivoire. The diversity of legal practices and religious backgrounds in the signatory nations affects the way people and organizations react to the new policies introduced under its influence.

Progressive laws promoting equality are frequently undermined in practice due to persistent discriminatory attitudes and institutional incapacity (Rohrs and Smythe 2014). Some scholars believe that closing the gender gap in Africa is essential to achieving social justice and reducing poverty, but the multitude of legal systems offer many different angles for managing gender inequalities (Kuenyehia 1998, xv). Women and other vulnerable categories are sometimes adversely affected by traditional or religious laws, or they do not make use of progressive legal structures because accessing and navigating these new systems can be difficult. Ignorance of the law is understandable when the coexistence of multiple legal systems complicates the administration of justice. Often policy and government law might not be widely practiced as customary law persists outside of urban centers and is supported by some traditional and religious groups. Customary law and religious law often favor men in terms of access to land and therefore to economic opportunity (xviii). For example, in the case of Côte d'Ivoire, we have seen that although polygamy and the paying of bride price were outlawed by the colonial state, their legitimacy is still widespread at the grassroots level.

Progressive legislation falls short of promoting gender equality when other barriers continue to prevent its proper implementation (Rohrs and Smythe 2014)—particularly when this legislation falls into the hegemonic traps so typical of contemporary human rights reform. Power dynamics shape gender reforms. The data analyzed in the preceding chapters consistently shows that local responses to hegemonic modernity are multiple and fragmented. They are determined by power relationships as well as by the vested interests of various stakeholders. Figure 5.1 captures both the reality of legal pluralism and the hierarchical relationships between different legal systems inherent in gender reform processes.

This section highlights the "unequal but mutually constitutive legal orders" connected to the following questions posed by Sally Merry:

Figure 5.1.   Gender reform stakeholders

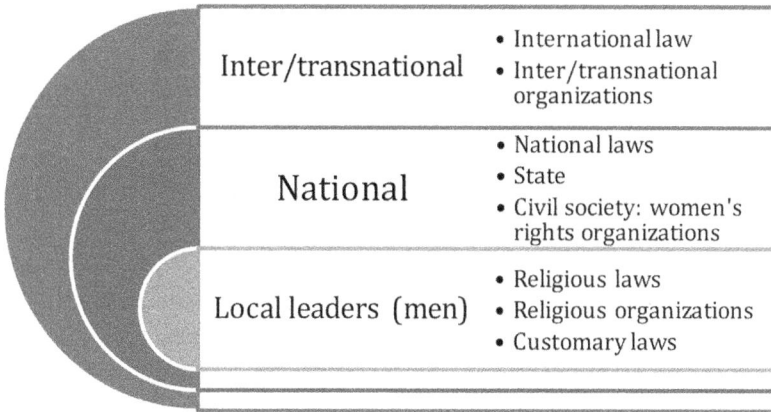

Inter/transnational	• International law • Inter/transnational organizations
National	• National laws • State • Civil society: women's rights organizations
Local leaders (men)	• Religious laws • Religious organizations • Customary laws

Source: Author

"How do these systems interact and reshape one another? To what extent is the dominant system able to control the subordinate ones? How do subordinate systems subvert or evade the dominant system? Are there ways in which the competing strategies of subordinate users reshape the dominant system? To what extent do contests among plural legal systems explain historical change?" (1992, 358). As the regional and comparative perspectives introduced in chapter 4 indicate, the scenario varies from one country to another. Even if the state remains the central player in the process of vernacularization of global women's rights, local leaders, depending on their influence, can successfully stall the process of gender reform. In other words, in spite of the enormous power of the international enforcement regime, every state still must contend with the power structure of its own local politics. When under pressure from international or transnational organizations, the state tends to collaborate with women's rights groups, which operate as mediators in the process of vernacularization. Sally Merry notes that such mediators are a "key dimension" of the vernacularization process, translating "the discourses and practices from the arena of international law and legal institutions to specific situations of suffering and violation" and working "to negotiate between local, regional, national, and global systems of meanings" (Merry 2006, 39; see also Breton-Le Goff 2013). The failure or success of intermediaries' reform initiatives depends partly on the level of the resistance of local leaders and partly on the capacity of the state to contain them.

Although some early colonial legal reforms aimed at bettering the condition of women, gender concerns were not central to the early processes of modernizing Africa, which focused predominantly on economic development, largely perceived as a male activity. Larry Grubbs explains it in the following way:

> Inheriting colonial anthropological representations of African women as helpless and oppressed victims of patriarchy, Western development experts in the 1950s–60s (typically white men, of course) "overwhelmingly lumped women in post-colonial societies with the peasantry as repositories of tradition and potential obstacles to their transformative schemes." . . . Women were seen as loyal not to the nation or state, but to their family and community only. These gendered assumptions translated into development policies that privileged men and their involvement in the modern economy. Modernization planners failed to include in their calculations women's contributions to subsistence farming and other activities. (2009, 71)

Male domination of women is often located within a more comprehensive moral code that seeks to legitimate the gerontocratic and patriarchal ideology. In most of Africa, for example, the argument goes that because men pay the bride wealth and then provide for their families, gender equality cannot be the basis of family relationships. But with men increasingly unable to provide a subsistence income for their families, "women take over a growing burden of responsibility and often claim more influence on family decisions" (Schulz 2003, 142; see also Cooper 2010). In addition, more young women are getting educated and becoming professionally and economically independent from their husbands. There is no doubt that gender power dynamics in Africa are changing and that the education of women seems to be one of the major driving factors. Yet these changing dynamics introduce a number of hegemonic traps, which illustrate subtle forms of western ideological domination.

HEGEMONIC TRAPS

The first hegemonic trap is theoretical and epistemological, as several authors have recently highlighted (Amadiume 2005; Arnfred et al. 2004; Bah 2015; Nnaemeka 2005; Oyewumi 2005b). Brigid Sackey, for example, notes that "Western theories, which are historic and culture specific, have been applied globally, and since the 1980s some African feminists have become supportive of the gender discourse in the West and are applying these gender theories without much recourse to the context in which they arose" (2006, 50). Gwendolyn Mikell has argued that there is an African feminism distinct from Western feminism: "The slowly emerging African feminism is distinctly heterosexual, pro-natal, and concerned with many 'bread, butter, culture, and power' issues. To this extent it parallels the recent growth of feminism in many other non-Western countries" (1997b, 4; see also Mikell 1995; Nnaemeka 2005). From a similar critical perspective, while acknowledging the patriarchal framework of Islamic societies, which subjects women's lives to men's authority, Leila Ahmed has cautioned against what she calls "colonial feminism." She suggests that Islamic revival and conservatism is in many respects "a response to the discourses of colonialism and the colonial attempt to undermine Islam and Arab culture and replace them with Western practices and beliefs" (1992, 236). Still, Ahmed argues, "what is needed now is not a response to the colonial and postcolonial assault on non-Western cultures . . . but a move beyond confinement within those terms altogether and a rejection or incorporation of Western, non-Western, and indigenous inventions, ideas, and institutions on the basis of their merit, not their tribe of origin" (236).

A second dimension of the hegemonic trap in policy making is religious. It is obvious that the framework of Islamic and Christian missions in Africa was predominantly hegemonic. Ironically, given the close collaboration between colonial powers and missionaries in the establishment of Western educational and health systems in Africa, religious institutions became one of the main matrices of modernization and westernization processes in most parts of sub-Saharan Africa (Rivière 1997). Here, the trap of epistemological hegemony is hardly avoidable. Viewed from the present context, it is evident that earlier versions of secularization theories, developed to account for Western societies, have failed to do justice to the fate of religion not only in non-Western regions of the world but also in the West (Hefner 1998, 85). There is no doubt that the colonization of Africa brought about some structural social differentiation by effectively distinguishing practices of religious institutions from those of political and economic institutions. But until now modernization has not resulted in the decline of religion in African societies. On the contrary, religion is booming on the African continent, resulting in a growing competition for control of public space and debates (Lasseur and Mayrargue 2011).

Studies have shown that religions can either enhance or limit women's agency (Becker 2007; Camara 2007; Hackett 2000; Malogne-Fer and Fer 2015; Parsitau 2012). Religions play a fundamental role in the production and legitimation of gender differentiations and inequalities. It is therefore no surprise that religion is one of the strongholds of resistance to gender reforms that challenge traditional norms of family and sexuality (Rochefort and Sanna 2013). Gender reforms are much easier to enact in societies where, in addition to the secularization of politics and the public sphere, the "secularization of the private sphere of individual consciousness" is also taking place, meaning the increasing "radical dissociation of private sexuality from religion and even from morality" (Casanova 2017, 59). This development, however, is nowhere to be found in the West African countries under consideration in this book, where religion continues to be used by conservatives to push back against gender reforms.

Hefner (1998) identified three major religious responses to modernity: conquest as an attempt to homogenize world views (holy war), separation as isolation from society, and acceptance of pluralism. Conservative religious forces often resort to cultural nationalism to mobilize their bases against social reforms. "In the Global South," Shahra Razavi and Anne Jenichen note, "the effort to promote universal human rights norms has often pitted women's rights advocates against those who use religion to resist cultural imperialism and Western-style individualism (which they claim is alien to their societies)" (2010, 046). In such a context, outright external intervention can be counterproductive, as religious forces tend to reposition themselves as the guardians of a morality threatened by morally decadent secularist movements (Heinen 2013).

A third dimension of the hegemonic trap in contemporary Africa policy is elitism, both external and internal. At the external level, it takes the shape of international pressures and conditionalities (Burnham 1991, Cox 1993, Morton 2007). To justify the reform of the family code in 2013, the Ivorian government invoked its international obligations — namely, the 1995 ratification of CEDAW, which subjected them to the scrutiny and pressure of international human rights bodies. Such a move shows one of the traps of the elitist interventionism of hegemonic modernities: many reforms are undertaken more to please international donors and to access funds than out of concern for the advancement of the cause of the reform itself. Sally Merry puts it in terms of the vulnerability of local translators: "Local leaders are often eager to appear compliant with human rights expectations while continuing to act in noncompliant ways. Following the form and language of human rights while ignoring local violations is a common practice for government leaders. Human rights translators, like development consultants, are often caught in the middle" (2006, 43).

Worth raising is the question of the sustainability of ideological reforms driven mainly by economic dependency and interests. The economic conditionality of some of these reforms is no secret, as their "elaboration has been strongly supported by international donor organizations" in negotiations with governments (Schulz 2003, 142). Some Ivorians alleged that the 2013 gender reform was rushed because the government had applied for Millennium Challenge Corporation funds, a US foreign assistance and development scheme, and access to these funds depended on the passage of the reform (Kouakou 2014). This is not implausible. Writing about economic conditionality in the gender field in Tanzania, Lange and Tjomsland remarked that, "In the 2010s, the UN, bilateral donors, and some INGOs started pushing for policy changes that a large percentage of the Tanzanian population, including many of the NGOs and parliamentarians, did not agree with: the right to abortion and the rights of LGBT persons. Several NGOs have been offered funds to work on the rights of sexual minorities but have not accepted them" (2014, 80). Requesting policy reforms as a condition for economic aid is an integral dimension of hegemonic modernities. These reforms can be economic, political, or cultural. But "the continued subordination of democracy and human rights by Western governments to other policy concerns such as economic self-interest not only undermines policy credibility and legitimacy, but also eventually impairs effectiveness" (Sadie 2002, 68; see also Gordon 1992).

At the national level, one of main weaknesses of the interventionist and elitist approach resides in the fact that a small governing elite decides for everybody on policies that will result in major sociocultural shifts. In the 2013 reform of the family code in Côte d'Ivoire, state officials did not consult the population and give them a chance to own the process. Rural areas were simply ignored, and even in urban settings there was no attempt to involve other stakeholders—not even women. In the case of Mali, Dorothea Schulz underlined the ambivalent attitudes of state actors in the Ministry for the Promotion of Women, Children, and the Family with regard to the reform by pointing out that "only a few magistrates and members of the Ministry of Justice wholeheartedly support[ed] the legislative reform" (Schulz 2003, 142). As a result, "official proclamations about the timeliness of the reform" inspired "considerable suspicion by the majority of the population" (144). The bottom line is that decrees by themselves—especially unpopular decrees—do not effect social change. On such matters, it is within the ability of the state to conduct an inclusive process, to bring all sectors of society to participate in and own the process of reform, to disseminate the content of the reforms, and to effectively enforce final decisions that make a difference in the lives of women.

Hegemonic modernities have multiple layers and operate in multiple arenas (international, national, subnational, local, etc.). At the international level, it is the hegemony of Western societies over African societies that is most notable, especially when major cultural reforms are promulgated in response to the threat of foreign aid withdrawal (Asongu and Nwachukwu 2017); also notable is the hegemony of Western feminists over African feminists regarding theoretical innovations and policy orientation. At the national level, taking into account the fact that "marginalized and submerged groups such as rural women and minority groups lack the means, organization, and power to articulate their positions in national human rights" (Ibhawoh 2000, 851; Jeppie, Moosa, and Roberts 2010b; Hodgson 2017; Maoulidi 2017), occurs the hegemony of educated urban elites over rural farmers and herders, of men over women, of educated urban women over rural women, of male religious leaders over predominantly female believers, etc. The ruling elite, both political and religious, which is predominantly male, ends up deciding what is best for women.

I suggest a more differentiated democratic approach to gender reform, whereby after a formal phase of deliberation that involves all sectors of society, gender issues that significantly affect the lives of women are left to women to decide through a democratic process. Final decisions should not be the business of the international community, state officials, or religious clerics, but of women themselves.

Women's organizations have an important role to play as leaders and mediators in this process. Women's organizations have been at the forefront of the mobilization for gender reforms in Africa since independence in the early 1960s (Mikell 1995). Before colonization, women organized in groups for multiple social purposes, but the orientation of these groups was reshaped as women's social roles changed under European influence in Africa (Amadiume 1997, 177). The colonial and postcolonial era saw growth in women's councils and societies, many of which played a part in movements of political independence and democratization. These groups made their own rules, chose their members and leaders, and devised their strategies; yet, while still under colonial and patriarchal systems, they used symbols of male power and sometimes imitated masculine roles to achieve legitimacy (164). Women's organizations sought to promote female leadership in male-dominated societies. There has been a modern trend toward women's involvement in political power, and women's activism contributes to the creation of a robust civil society (Ampofo, Bekou-Betts, Njambi, and Osirim 2004, 704). The Association of African Women for Research and Development, for example, was created in 1977 to pursue "an agenda for African feminism through scholarship and activism" (686). In Cameroon, the Takumbeng women's movement in the 1990s displayed women's leadership potential as members spread information, condemned injustice with public marches, monitored election processes, and promoted overall democratic efforts within the state (Fonchingong and Tanga 2007, 136). Ivorian women grew more active under Islamic revivalism, and the 2002 military conflict saw more women-led groups emerge to settle disputes within religious parameters, while also focusing on women's health and education (LeBlanc 2014, 168).

In more recent years, democratization efforts have pushed for increases in women's political participation, although overwhelming gender disparities remain (Coffe and Bolzendhal 2011, 245). Men are significantly more involved than women in demonstrations, contacting officials, and party membership, and women tend to be excluded from leadership roles, resource mobilization, and public politics (246–47). Women, burdened with house and care work, are further constrained by employment, education, and marital and parental status, and are thus less available for political participation than men. Moreover, gender roles seep into early socialization, gearing girls toward a more passive and private role while orienting boys toward leadership and autonomy. One study found that women in nations like Benin and Senegal are much less likely to register to vote, a factor tied to differences in socioeconomic status (253). The relationship between gender and politics is complex, yet it is evident that progress is being made toward inclusiveness, especially as more women have access to quality education.

One persistent issue affecting the relationship between religion, the state, and gender in Africa is legal pluralism. The family unit is central to belief systems. Therefore, the regulation of the roles of each family member is of religious, as much as legal, importance (Jeppie, Moosa, and Roberts 2010a, 22). In fact, in some West African countries, the law of the state was or still is religious, as is the case where Muslim law is applied (Camara 2007). Colonial policies focused on regulating the family because its stability was understood to be crucial to overall stability in the colony; thus, European secular legal orders attempted to subvert local customary and religious practice in dealing with community and family disputes. But eventually colonial powers settled for a situation of legal pluralism, allowing concurrent legal systems to operate in many African societies (Jeppie, Moosa, and Roberts 2010a, 23). The overlap between customary law, religious law, and European law made for a complex system of justice and complicated people's relationships within the social order. Colonial courts only dealt with certain disputes, while others were settled in native courts using both traditional and religious jurisprudence or through informal dispute resolution. Each system had a main focus. Islamic law, for example, generally regulated marriage, divorce, inheritance, and family matters in francophone Africa, while the colonial state oversaw its implementation (49). Politicized gender relations were shaped by courts influenced by a European patriarchal model, and men became the dominant actors for the family, while women were often subjugated in areas of social and public life. Thus, legal systems had palpable effects on the role religion played in society, as well as on how community members interacted and accessed power.

I have argued in this section that on the issue of gender reform in West African countries, women are confronted with both external (international) and internal (national) hegemonic systems of decision-making that deprive them of the final say over decisions that affect their lives. The workings of hegemonic modernities are found not only in the relationships between non-Western societies and the West, which is the center of production of dominant cultural ideologies, but also in relations between the dominant elites and the dominated sections of the population within African societies. In the next section of this chapter, building on my critique of hegemonic approaches to gender reform in West Africa, I suggest that policy making on gender issues could benefit from a more dialogical and intercultural framework.

INTERCULTURALITY AND POLICY MAKING: TOWARD A DIALOGICAL FRAMEWORK

Culture is a battlefield in contemporary international relations (Harshe 2006), especially around the diplomacy of human rights (Ruggie 1983). In the promotion of gender equality, culture and religions are often portrayed as obstacles to women's rights in non-Western societies. Cultural and religious practices such as female genital mutilation and girl-child marriage are widely portrayed as harmful to women and are major targets of planned change in many parts of Africa. Bonny Ibha-woh addressed the question of the "cultural legitimacy" of human rights, inquiring "into the kinds and degrees of support for human rights standards and for their implementation in culture(s), be it 'micro-cultures' of villages or tribes, or 'subcultures' of professions and social classes, or 'national cultures,' or 'regional cultures'" (2000, 840). The question is how to reconcile African cultural traditions with the social norms often projected as universal by the liberal democracies of the

West—how to ground universal notions of human rights in a community narrative to give these values cultural legitimacy in the eyes of Africans.

How to reconcile human rights with traditional cultures? Two considerations are important in answering this question. First, the constitutions of many African countries stipulate that the rights they guarantee cannot be violated on the grounds of customary or religious law. Second, culture is dynamic and can change. African cultures, like others, are dynamic and ever changing. But while social scientists agree that culture changes, they don't necessarily agree on how it changes or on how to effect cultural change. To try to combat loss of African culture by attempting to inhibit change is to mistake natural pathways of cultural dynamism for assimilation. It would be a mistake to allow the particularly violent nature of the colonial encounter to instill an unnecessary wariness toward change.

Still, Bonny Ibhawoh has argued that ensuring the cultural legitimacy of any legal human rights reform is key to its implementation. He distinguished two main competing cultural legitimacy paradigms in Africa: the conservative paradigm, which he associates with the urban-based male elite, and the dynamic paradigm, associated with women's organizations and civil society organizations (2000, 850). This is a helpful mapping of social forces that either enhance or impede the promotion of human rights in Africa, although, as the data analyzed for this book shows, each of these paradigms recruits both men and women. Bonny Ibhawoh seems to suggest that because cultures are part of the problem, they should also be part of the solution. To build local ownership of reform, he advocates for dialogue between the major paradigms of cultural legitimacy that coexist within a particular society:

It is important to create dialogue between weaker and stronger groups within the cultural community and society at large. Women and minority groups must be able to dialogue over interpretations of cultural values with politicians, officials, traditional leaders, and family heads in both the rural and urban areas. If respect for human rights is to be achieved and made sustainable, human rights must reside not only in law but in the living and practiced culture of the people. There is a need, therefore, for dialogue among groups with different paradigms of culture on what role culture should play in legitimizing national human rights regimes within African states. What is advocated is some form of "cross-paradigmatic" approach to the quest for national consensus on the way to enhance cultural legitimacy. (855)

Even in this dialogical framework, any cultural reform should be left up to local communities. In this respect, the burden also falls on Western women—who may, perhaps rightfully, see themselves as advocates for all women—to avoid insensitivity toward cultural contexts with which they are not familiar. Ultimately, this book is concerned with the potential for backlash from local communities, should they feel robbed of their status as stakeholders.

It is therefore critical to avoid the trap of promoting globally standardized human values that may deprive African nations of the ability to chart their own cultural futures, for better or for worse. If local political leaders are provided an opportunity to construe undesirable social agendas as Western (or perhaps secular) encroachment on local values, well-meaning advocates and NGOs run the risk of creating situations that are ultimately damaging to the groups they intend to help. In no sphere does this appear to be truer than in the ongoing debate on the place (or lack thereof) of homosexuality in African societies. A recent study on the subject concluded, "We find that foreign aid distortions as a policy instrument for the promotion of political rights is a considerable policy reversal because it brings about the opposite effect of the intended" (Asongu and Nwachukwu 2017, 213). "The simple answer" to why this is the case, according to M. Ssenyonjo, "is that cultural obstacles in Africa are deeply entrenched and most states have not adopted immediate and effective measures, particularly in the fields of teaching, education and information, to combat discrimination against women." Thus, African states must "give urgent attention to the general duty of states to modify the social and cultural patterns of conduct of women and men through public education" (2007, 65). Education has indeed proven to be a major driver of social change in Africa, but it takes time for education to change beliefs and practices. The time factor is a major challenge for policymakers, who are constantly tempted to resort to quick-fix solutions.

According to Eisenstadt (2000), inherent in the project of modernity, including its Western version, are irreducible tensions between universalism and pluralism, individualism and collectivism, cosmopolitanism and localism, multifaceted identities and closed identities, and essentialism and relativism. At the heart of the domestication of hegemonic modernities in Africa is the struggle to find a healthy balance between the good of the community and the good of the individual. The concept of "ubuntu," which translates as "humanness," encapsulates in African philosophy the communalism of African traditional societies (Enslin and Horsthemke 2004; Lutz 2009). Ubuntu philosophy seeks to prioritize the interests of the community in a way that still serves the interests of the individual (Bongmba 2004). By contrast, as Eisenstadt rightly remarked, the cornerstone of Western modernity is the autonomy of man (2000, 5). In many modern Western ideologies, this autonomy is construed as individualism that celebrates the primacy of individual rights and interests.

On these issues of individualism and community, it is important to acknowledge that African societies and Western societies operate differently. Since the beginning of colonization, African societies have been negotiating their transition from community-oriented societies to individual-oriented societies. In spite of the globalization of culture, the debate about human rights that seeks to contrast "Western liberal individualism" with "African, Asian, and Islamic collectivist communitarianism" is far from over. S. K. Hellsten argues: "In this debate, the communitarian position seems to equate liberal, individualistic promotion of universal values with cultural assimilation that results in the fragmentation and demise of various traditional cultures. Liberal individualists, on the other hand, blame communitarian relativism for its oppressive tendencies and conservatism towards those minorities who do not agree with the commonly adopted values and social norms" (2010, 37–38).

I caution against overemphasizing the dichotomy between an individualistic West and a communitarian non-West, because the debate between communitarianism and individualism is also a major component of Western political thought (Hollenbach 2002; Kymlicka 1995; Nozick 1974; Rawls 1971, 1993; Sandel 1982, 1984). But the promotion of gender equality in Africa is undeniably part of the agenda to spread the more liberal Western perspective on human rights beyond the West (Ferguson 2006). Resistance to the neoliberal agenda in the name of traditional values is not specific to non-Western countries. Kristina Stoeckl (2014), for example, writes of the Russian Orthodox Church's resistance to "liberal hegemony."

The colonial project failed to positively transform Africa largely because of its hegemonic framework. Imposed cultural engineering is violence. The failure of colonization as a figure of hegemonic modernity has sufficiently proven that what is best for the West is not necessarily best for the rest of the world. A universal culture does not exist, but it can be constructed out of a healthy dialogue of particular cultures. No culture is perfect, and no culture is static. Outside actors should never force a community to change its values because they think they know what is good for them. At best, they can initiate dialogue with the community in the hope of convincing them to initiate its own process of altering cultural practices and values. This dialogical and deliberative approach privileges working toward a consensus. Penny Enslin and Kai Horsthemke explain that "to be legitimate, deliberation must be strongly egalitarian, allowing all affected by a decision to initiate discussion, to influence its agenda and to question its procedures." All cultural traditions "include features that sit in tension with the demands of democracy," and for this reason "democratic principles require that citizens participate on free and equal terms in debating the future of traditions and practices of their society." Education prepares citizens for this deliberation, and the capacity to deliberate empowers citizens to decide for themselves "the extent to which they wish to define themselves in traditional terms." Suppressing such debate "by fixing political identities and practices according to an Africanist script is in itself an undemocratic device," as is "excluding from the debate ideas that are western or liberal on the pretext that they are not appropriate to Africa" (Enslin and Horsthemke 2004, 552, 556; see also Benhabib 1996; Murithi 2009).

To escape the hegemonic trap that has distorted modernization efforts in Africa, gender reforms should be relocated within the framework of an intercultural dialogue that is respectful of the will and rhythm of each group involved. If gender identities are indeed socially and culturally constructed, they cannot be constructed in the same way everywhere. A mutually challenging intercultural dialogue provides an avenue for genuine conversation between two different cultures. What can the non-Western world learn from the emphasis on individual freedom, and, vice versa, what can the Western world learn from the emphasis on community values? Different cultures can share best practices and learn from one another. It is not a matter of choosing between the community and the individual, because both belong together. The result is a healthy balance between the good of the community and the freedom of the individual—probably one of the major challenges of the modern world (Taylor 1992). In democracy, significant cultural reforms should be predicated on significant consultation with the people concerned and should not run counter to their will. Hegemonic approaches to gender reform have created situations in which women themselves oppose reforms that are purportedly destined to improve their condition. Any attempt to force people to change their culture will not only provoke conflict, it will be bound to fail. That is why education, in spite of having its own hegemonic trappings in Africa, has proven to be a much more effective tool to transform gender dynamics (Pickbourn and Ndikumana 2016) than well-meaning legal reforms carried out without significant consultation with the people at the grassroots.

Modern Africa is not witnessing the unchallenged triumph of liberalism (Fukuyama 1992). Nor is it the arena of an outward "clash of civilizations" (Huttington 1996) between liberalism and traditional cultures. Liberal democracy and capitalism have made some inroads in Africa, but it is not yet possible to speak of their triumph on the continent. The spread of the culture of neoliberalism in the area of gender, family, and sexuality has been met with fierce resistance in some conservative circles. The major question in this battle for gender equality remains: Is what is best for the West necessarily the best for Africa? The answer to this question should ultimately be left to Africans themselves. Hegemonic modernities have consistently failed to do just that.

Conclusion

Religion, the State, and Gender Reform in Sub-Saharan Africa

By way of conclusion, I focus on the dynamic relationship between religion and politics in contemporary Africa. I locate the debate about religion and gender politics within the wider framework of the role of religion in the public sphere in Africa (Casanova 1994; Englund 2012; Lado 2012). In doing so, I attempt to contribute to the debate on the workings of secularization in modern Africa, which in many respects is still a profoundly religious continent.

Saskia Van Hoyweghen (1996) has argued that to see postcolonial African societies as becoming increasingly and necessarily secular overlooks and oversimplifies key aspects of religious practice and meaning on the continent. Although the colonial legacy of the secular state is conducive to religious pluralism in Africa, it has not resulted in separation between religion and politics, partly because religion is still largely considered the ultimate source of power (Abbink 2014; Ellis and Ter Haar 1998; Hinfelaar 2012). Church-state relationships vary depending on the political history and religious demographics of a country (Akoko and Oben 2006; Boyle 1992; Hinfelaar 2012; Van Hoyweghen 1996). Recent history has seen conflict between the religious and the secular in a number of African countries, for example in the nationalization of mission schools and health services or the exclusion of religion from academic curricula in public schools. But religion as a cultural force continues to shape both public debate and private engagement with politics in Africa. It follows that in the study of contemporary Africa, "to ignore religion, as a matter of obvious political and even economic importance, threatens the credibility of academic investigations" (Bompani and Frahm-Arp 2010, 7; see also Ellis and Ter Haar 1998).

Notwithstanding secularization processes and debates, "religion in Africa was never relegated, even superficially, to a space outside politics and current events, or to benign places of private worship." On the contrary, "religion has always been perceived, by Africans, as having the power to radically change social life and history" (Smith 2012, 2). Performing alongside civil society organizations, religions in Africa, especially Christianity and Islam, are very active in the provision of social services, in public debates related to human rights, in social justice, and in the promotion of democratic culture (Gifford 1998, 2015; see also Chikwendu 2004; Gary 2002; Trinitapoli 2006). The public manifestation of religion in Africa takes many forms, including calls to prayer, posters advertising religious events, religious performances in the media, and religious buildings mushrooming in city suburbs, among others.

Afrobarometer data from 2012 found that religious leaders are generally held in higher regard than any other type of leader or public official in Africa (Manglos and Weinreb 2013). Political leaders therefore try to be perceived as religious, and candidates often appeal to religious communities to mobilize voters, create clientele, or organize constituencies (Ellis and Ter Haar 1998; 2007). Yet political elites are not simply manipulating religion as a means to increase support; many of them do believe that access to the spiritual world provides essential and real power. A study using data from thirteen African nations found that active religious membership positively shapes political interest in most countries (Manglos and Weinreb 2013). Widespread disappointment in the political system, moreover, has made religious spheres the preferred spaces for social protest and the fight for change, as religion is understood as an instrumental tool to enrich the public sphere and motivate people. Religion and politics both regulate power in society, but these forces relate to people in different ways. The inclusive potential of religion, as opposed to the divisiveness of politics, provides a space for effective dialogue and connects individuals to larger power spheres (Manglos and Weinreb 2013, 199).

Today, however, the active presence of religion in the public sphere is becoming a challenge for public authorities. Missionary Christianity used to be the only major religious actor in the public space in sub-Saharan Africa, partly because Christian schools provided the first generations of civil servants who took over from the colonial administration. But things are rapidly changing, with competing religious groups vying for some share of the public space directly through politics, social action, and social debates (Gomez-Perez 2005; Miran-Guyon 2006). In recent decades, for example, Pentecostal Christianity has expanded rapidly in most of sub-Saharan Africa, leading to competition and obvious tensions with missionary Christianity in many areas, including a battle for membership and a share of the public space. In West Africa, some groups within the Muslim elite have also become very vocal in public debates, especially on issues pertaining to public morality and gender reforms. Some Muslim clerics complain about what they perceive as subtle attempts to impose a Western secular agenda incompatible with Islamic values (Soares 2005). Some of the issues that have sparked heated debates in the aftermath of the 1990s liberalization trend include the opening of bars during Ramadan, the spread of brothels, gambling, the distribution of pornographic material, gender equality, female circumcision, beauty pageants, homosexuality, the use of condoms, and family code reforms.

In the history of West Africa, religion has played a key role in shaping gender norms that govern social order and control. Amadiume (1997) argues that in many parts of precolonial Africa, gender distinctions functioned less to establish male domination over women and more to direct the division of labor, meaning that political and economic systems were cooperatively managed. Particularly in matrilineal societies, the importance of the mother figure made women more prominent, and women could engage in the public sphere, in economic transactions, and in religious ceremonies. In many African traditional settings, women were key religious players (Hackett 2000). However, this more flexible system seems to have eroded over time, in favor of a more rigid and polarized gendered politics attributed by critics to the influence of new religions and colonization (Camara 2007; Mikell 1997a). The traditional roles of men and women within society and religion were reshaped fundamentally. The male became the sole sphere for power, subordinating the female and undoing a history of powerful African women (Amadiume 1997, 146).

Religious movements react to globalization, consumerism, and technological changes in ways that affect individual and collective identities (Frahm-Arp 2008, 86). Family dynamics and political affiliation are often shaped by religion as belief systems direct how interactions between genders, classes, and races should be arranged (88). Religious movements provide structure, meaning, and belonging while shaping and adapting to social norms and cultural change. We are dealing with a continent where the role of religion is multifaceted, powerful, and, to some degree, up for grabs. State actors attempt to harness its power and, in turn, find themselves forced to respond and adapt to that power. Religion is deeply and inextricably linked to identity formation and personal values, but religious voices are left out of debates and policy changes that explicitly seek to intervene on those values. This contribution on gender policy in Côte d'Ivoire makes it clear that a top-down reform to family law without attention to religious stakeholders or religious belief has very little chance of affecting significant change to gender equality in Africa. It is an example that points quite clearly to the limits of legal reform that fails to attend to either social practice or to its religious and cultural underpinnings.

NOTES

Introduction

1. Law No. 2015–635 of September 17, 2015, was a modification of Law No. 95–696 of September 7, 1995, on education. It requires boys and girls to attend school through age sixteen.

ONE. The Secular State in the 2013 Gender Reform in Côte d'Ivoire

1. I would like to acknowledge the important contribution of Mr. Boris Glodé, research assistant, who did the background press review and organized the data used in this chapter. See Glodé 2019.

2. The primary data used in this chapter is based on a review of the Ivorian printed press, which gives an idea of the chronology of events and the terms of political maneuvers. In the Ivorian context, there is only one major newspaper officially positioned as a government mouthpiece: *Fraternité Matin*. Other newspapers perceived as allies of the government are *Le Patriote*, *Le Nouveau réveil*, and *Le Jour Plus*. Among the newspapers associated with opposition parties, *Le Temps*, *Notre Voie*, and *Le Courrier d'Abidjan* were consulted for this book. Newspapers not explicitly linked to political parties include *Soir Info* and *L'Inter*.

3. After nearly ten years of prosecution at the International Criminal Court, Laurent Gbagbo was acquitted and returned to Abidjan in June 2021.

4. In 2016, Yasmina Ouégnin was reelected for the municipality of Cocody, but this time as an independent candidate after falling out with her party.

TWO.   Negotiating Multiplicity

1. That codification consisted of eight laws adopted on October 7, 1964: Law No. 64–373 on naming, Law No. 64–374 on civil status, Law No. 64–375 on marriage, Law No. 64–376 on divorce and legal separation, Law No. 64–377 on paternity and affiliation, Law No. 64–378 on adoption, Law No. 64–379 on inheritance, and Law No. 64–380 on donations by the living and the will. In the overview that follows, I am indebted to Dr. Gilles Kragbe's detailed analysis of the history of the reform of the family code in Côte d'Ivoire, recently published as Kragbe 2019.

2. Article 10 of Law No. 64–381 of October 7, 1964.

3. Since the passage of the 1983 family law, those dispensations are decided by the state prosecutor.

4. Law No. 64–375 of October 7, 1964, Article 68.

5. For this study, SDEF-Afrique collected data and helped draft the preliminary report; their work forms the basis of this section. I wish to thank Mrs. Edith Behibro, who heads SDEF-Afrique, for her support and input. A French version of the data used in this chapter is published as Behibro 2019.

FOUR.   Regional and Comparative Perspectives

1. Sufism, the mystical tradition of Islam, has a strong religious presence throughout West Africa, where it is firmly rooted in local cultures. The Sufi Islamic brotherhoods, such as the Qadiriyya, the Tijaniyya, and the Muridiyya, are of great religious and sociopolitical importance and continue to be spiritual, intellectual, and social forces in many countries in West Africa.

2. For the chronology of events in this section, the author is indebted to Fatou Sarr's paper presented at the Centre de Recherche et d'Action pour Paix (CERAP) workshop held on June 1–2, 2016, entitled "Du code de la famille de 1972 à la loi sur la parité de 2010 au Sénégal." It is published as Sarr 2019.

3. The brotherhood of the Mourides is the biggest within Sufi Islam in Senegal. It was founded in the nineteenth century and accommodated many local traditional practices. Its leaders exert considerable political influence in the country.

4. Women still complain about the partial application of that law today. The opinion of many women is that the present government has not re-

spected the provisions of the law, as the number of appointed women falls below the legal quota; only eight women feature in a government of forty-two ministers (Alio 2005).

5. For the sequence of events in this narrative, the author relied heavily on Samaké 2019.

6. Excerpt from a document of the secretary general of the Islamic Council presented at the debriefing meeting after the adoption of the family law on August 9, 2009.

REFERENCES

Abbink, J. 2014. "Religion and Politics in Africa: The Future of 'the Secular.'" *AfricaSpectrum* 3:83–106.

Abitbol, E. 1966. "La famille conjugale et le droit nouveau du mariage en Côte d'Ivoire." *Journal of African Law* 10 (3): 141–63.

Agence Nationale de la Statistique et de la Démographie. 2014. Data of General Population Census of 2013. http://www.ansd.sn/ressources/RG PHAE-2013/ressources/doc/pdf/2.pdf. Accessed Oct. 29, 2019.

Ahmed, L. 1992. *Women and Gender in Islam*. New Haven, CT: Yale University Press.

Ajulu, R. 2001. "Thabo Mbeki's African Renaissance in a Globalising World Economy: The Struggle for the Soul of the Continent." *Review of African Political Economy* 28 (87): 27–42.

Akoko, R. M., and T. M. Oben. 2006. "Christian Churches and the Democratization Conundrum in Cameroon." *Africa Today* 52 (3): 25–48.

Akwaba, S. C. 2012. "Dissolution du gouvernement, loi sur le mariage, accusation entrealliés: Qui a trahi qui?" *Le Nouveau Réveil* 3239 (Nov. 16): 3–5.

Alidou, O. 2005. *Engaging Modernity: Muslim Women and the Politics of Agency in Postcolonial Niger*. Madison: University of Wisconsin Press.

Alidou, O., and H. Alidou. 2008. "Women, Religion, and the Discourses of Legal Ideology in Niger Republic." *Africa Today* 54 (3): 21–36.

Alio, M. 2005. "Une révolution avortée: Le code de la famille au Niger." In *Actes du colloque: Quel droit de la famille pour le Niger?*, 167–82. Niamey, Niger: Universite Abdou Moumouni; Institut Danois des Droits de L'Homme (IDDH).

Amadiume, I. 1997. *Reinventing Africa: Matriarchy, Religion, and Culture*. London: Zed Books.

———. 2005. "Theorizing Matriarchy in Africa: Kinship Ideologies and Systems in Africa and in Europe." In *African Gender Studies: A Reader*, edited by E. Oyewumi, 83–98. New York: Palgrave Macmillan.

Ampofo, A. A., J. Bekou-Betts, W. N. Njambi, and M. Osirim. 2004. "Women's and Gender Studies in English-Speaking Sub-Saharan Africa: A Review of Research in the Social Sciences." *Gender and Society* 18 (6): 685–714.

Anderson, J. N. D., ed. 1968. *Family Law in Asia and Africa*. London: Allen and Unwin.

Appleby, S. 2012. Foreword to *Displacing the State: Religion and Conflict in Neoliberal Africa*, edited by J. H. Smith and R. I. J. Hackett, vii–x. Notre Dame, IN: University of Notre Dame Press.

Arnfred, S., B. Bakare-Yusuf, E. W. Kisiang'ani, D. Lewis, O. Oyewumi, and F. C. Steady. 2004. *African Gender Scholarship: Concepts, Methodologies, and Paradigms*. Dakar, Senegal: Codesria Books.

Asongu, S. A., and J. C. Nwachukwu. 2017. "Is the Threat of Foreign Aid Withdrawal an Effective Deterrent to Political Oppression? Evidence from Fifty-Three African Countries." *Journal of Economic Issues* 51 (1): 201–21.

Augis, E. 2012. "Religion, Religiousness, and Narrative: Decoding Women's Practices in Senegalese Islamic Reform." *Journal for the Scientific Study of Religion* 51 (3): 29–441.

Awonko, P. 2012. "Médias, politique et homosexualité au Cameroun: Retour sur la construction d'une controverse." *Politique Africaine* 126:69–86.

Bah, M. 2015. *Le genre dans l'historiographie de l'Afrique de l'ouest et du centre*. Dakar, Senegal: Codesria Books.

Bahi, M. A. 2014. "The Justice System and Women's Rights in Côte d'Ivoire." In *In Search of Equality: Women, Law, and Society in Africa*, edited by S. Rohrs, D. Smythe, A. Hsieh, and M. de Souza, 148–70. Cape Town: University of Cape Town Press.

Becker, C., ed. 2007. *Genre, inégalités et religion: Actes du premier colloque inter-réseaux du programme thématique "Aspects de l'État de droit et démocratie," Dakar, 25–27 Avril 2006*. Agence universitaire de la Francophonie. Paris: Éditions des Archives Contemporaines.

Behibro, E. 2019. "Le marriage civil dans le district d'Abidjan de 2013 à 2017." In *État, Religion et Genre en Afrique Occidentale et Centrale*, edited by L. Lado and R. Yao Gnabeli, 269–86. Bamenda, Cameroon: Langaa RPCIG.

Bela, E. 2012. "Projet de loi sur la famille en Côte d'Ivoire: L'agréable avant l'utile." *Chronique des Temps Nouveaux*, Dec. 19, 2–5.

Benhabib, S. 1996. "Toward a Deliberative Model of Democratic Legitimacy." In *Democracy and Difference: Contesting the Boundaries of the Political*, edited by S. Benhabib, 67–94. Princeton, NJ: Princeton University Press.

Benjamin, H. 1966. *The Transsexual Phenomenon*. New York: Julian Press.

Boga, S. 2012a. "Ouassénan à Bédié: Vous etes le responsable de ce que nous vivons." *Notre Voie*, no. 4276 (Nov. 23): 2–4.

———. 2012b. "Le PDCI recule." *Notre Voie*, no. 4275 (Nov. 16): 3–5.

Bompani, B., and M. Frahm-Arp. 2010. "Development and Politics from Below: New Conceptual Interpretations." Introduction to *Development and Politics from Below: Exploring Religious Spaces in the African State*, edited by B. Bompani and M. Frahm-Arp, 1–22. New York: Palgrave Macmillan.

Bongmba, E. K. 2004. "Reflections on Thabo Mbeki's African Renaissance." *Journal of Southern African Studies* 30 (2): 291–316.

Boserup, E. 1983. *La femme face au développement économique*. Paris: PUF.

Bourdieu, P. 2014. *La domination masculine*. Paris: Seuil.

Boye, A. K., K. Hill, S. Isaacs, and D. Gordis. 1991. "Marriage Law and Practice in the Sahel." *Studies in Family Planning* 22 (6): 343–49.

Boyle, P. M. 1992. "Beyond Self-Protection to Prophecy: The Catholic Church and Political Change in Zaire." *Africa Today* 39 (3): 49–66.

Brenner, L. 1993. "La culture Arabo-Islamique au Mali." In *Le radicalisme Islamique au Sud du Sahara*, edited by R. Otayek, 161–96. Paris: Karthala.

Breton-Le Goff, G. 2013. "Aux confins du droit positif: Socio-anthropologie de la production normative non gouvernementale en République démocratique du Congo." *Anthropologie et Sociétés* 37 (1): 75–95.

Broqua, C. 2012. "L'émergence des minorités sexuelles dans l'espace public en Afrique." *Politique Africaine* 126 (2): 5–23.

Brossier, M. 2004. "Les débats sur le droit de la famille au Sénégal: Une mise enquestion des fondements de l'autorité légitime?" *Politique Africaine* 96 (4): 78–98.

Burnham, P. 1991. "Neo-Gramscian Hegemony and the International Order." *Capital and Class* 15 (3): 73–92.

Butler, J. 1990. *Gender Trouble: Feminism and the Politics of Subversion*. New York: Routledge.

Camara, F. K. 2007. "Le code de la famille du Sénégal ou de l'utilisation de la religion comme alibi à la légalisation de l'inégalité de genre." In *Genre, Inégalités et Religion*, edited by C. Becker, 163–83. Paris: Éditions des Archives Contemporaines.

Casanova, J. 1994. *Public Religions in the Modern World*. Chicago: University of Chicago Press.

———. 2017. "Catholicism, Gender, Secularism, and Democracy: Comparative Reflections." In *Islam, Gender, and Democracy in Comparative Perspective*, edited by J. Cesari and J. Casanova, 46–62. New York: Oxford University Press.

Castelli, E. A. 2001. "Women, Gender, Religion: Troubling Categories and Transforming Knowledge." In *Women, Gender, Religion: A Reader*, edited by E. A. Castelli, 3–21. New York: Palgrave.

Chevalier, J. 2005. *Genre et développement au Bénin: L'évolution des conditions de la femme des années 80 à aujourd'hui.* Montréal: Université du Québec à Montréal.

Chikwendu, E. 2004. "Faith-Based Organizations in Anti-HIV/AIDS Work among African Youth and Women." *Dialectical Anthropology* 28 (3/4): 307–27.

CIRCOFS. 2002. *Projet de code de statut personnel.* Dakar, Senegal: Institut Islamique de Dakar.

Clair, A. 1965. *Le Niger, pays à découvrir.* Paris: Hachette.

Coffe, H., and C. Bolzendahl. 2011. "Gender Gaps in Political Participation across Sub-Saharan African Nations." *Social Indicators Research* 102 (2): 245–64.

Conley, J. M., and W. M. O'Barr. 1993. "Legal Anthropology Comes Home: A Brief History of the Ethnographic Study of Law." *Loyola of Los Angeles Law Review* 27 (1):41–64.

Cooper, B. M. 2010. "Secular States, Muslim Law, and Islamic Religious Culture: Gender Implications of Legal Struggles in Hybrid Legal Systems in Contemporary West Africa." *Droit et cultures* 59 (1): 97–120. http://journals.openedition.org/droitcultures/1982. Accessed Oct. 29, 2019.

Cornwall, A. 2005. "Introduction: Perspectives on Gender in Africa." In *Readings in Gender in Africa*, edited by A. Cornwall, 1–19. London: International African Institute.

Cox, R. 1993. "Gramsci, Hegemony, and International Relations: An Essay in Method." In *Gramsci, Historical Materialism, and International Relations*, edited by S. Gill, 49–66. Cambridge: Cambridge University Press.

Croucher, S. 2002. "South Africa's Democratisation and the Politics of Gay Liberation." *Journal of Southern African Studies* 28 (2): 315–30.

Currier, A. 2010. "Political Homophobia in Postcolonial Namibia." *Gender and Society* 24: 110–29.

de Beauvoir, S. 1949. *Le deuxième sexe, tome 2: L'expérience vécue.* Paris: Gallimard.

Della Sudda, M., and G. Malochet. 2012. "Pouvoirs, genre et religions." *Travail, Genre et Sociétés* 27 (1): 29–32.

Demange, E. 2012. "De l'abstinence à la l'homophobie: 'La mobilisation' de la société Ougandaise, une ressource politique entre Ouganda et Etats-Unis." *Politique Africaine* 126:25–48.

Depry, D., and S. Boga. 2012. "Gouvernement Ouattara 2: Les vraies raisons d'une dissolution." *Notre Voie*, no. 4270 (Nov. 16): 2–3.

Deutsch, J.-G. 2002. "Introduction: Cherished Visions and Entangled Meanings." In *African Modernities*, edited by J.-G. Deutsch, P. Probst, and H. Schmidt, 1–17. Portsmouth, NH: Heinemann.

Diakité, M. 2016. "Situation juridique et avenir de la femme au Niger." *Revue Franco Maghrébine de Droit* 23:45–78.

Dlamini, J. 2015. "On Being in Time: Modern African Elites and the Historical Challenge to Claims for Alternative and Multiple Modernities." In *African, American, and European Trajectories of Modernity: Past Oppression, Future Justice?*, edited by P. Wagner, 64–76. Edinburgh: Edinburgh University Press.

Dunbar, A. R. 1991. "Islamic Values, the State, and the Development of Women: The Case of Niger." In *Hausa Women in the Twentieth Century*, edited by C. Coles and B. Mack, 69–89. Madison: University of Wisconsin Press.

Eisenstadt, S. N. 2000. "Multiple Modernities." *Daedalus* 129 (1): 1–29.

Ellis, S., and G. Ter Haar. 1998. "Religion and Politics in Sub-Saharan Africa." *Journal of Modern African Studies* 36 (2): 175–201.

———. 2007. "Religion and Politics: Taking African Epistemologies Seriously." *Journal of Modern African Studies* 45 (3): 385–401.

Ellovich, R. S. 1985. "The Law and Ivoirian Women." *Anthropos* 80:185–97.

Emane, J. 1967. "Les droits patrimoniaux de la femme mariée ivoirienne." *Annales Africaines*. Paris: Ed. Pedone.

Englund, H. 2012. "Rethinking African Christianities: Beyond the Religion-Politics Conundrum." In *Christianity and Public Culture in Africa*, edited by H. Englund, 1–24. Athens: Ohio University Press.

Enslin, P., and K. Horsthemke. 2004. "Can Ubuntu Provide a Model for Citizenship Education in African Democracies?" *Comparative Education* 40 (4): 545–58.

Epprecht, M. 2008. *Heterosexual Africa? The History of an Idea from the Age of Exploitation to the Age of AIDS*. Athens: Ohio University Press.

Esimai, C. 2007. "The Convergence of Local and International Law: Family Law in the Protocol on the Rights of Women in Africa." *American Society of International Law* 101:135–38.

Evans-Pritchard, E. E. 1970. "Sexual Inversion among the Azande." *American Anthropologist* 72 (6): 1428–34.

Ferguson, J. 2006. *Global Shadows: Africa in the Neoliberal World Order*. Durham, NC: Duke University Press.

Folquet, L. G. 1974. "La situation juridique de la femme mariée dans le nouveau droit de la famille Ivoirienne." *Revue juridique et politique indépendante et cooperation*, 636–37. Paris: Ediafric.

Fonchingong, C., and P. Tanga. 2007. "Crossing Rural-Urban Spaces: The 'Takumbeng' and Activism in Cameroon's Democratic Crusade." *Cahiers d'Etudes Africaines* 47 (185): 117–43.

Frahm-Arp, M. 2008. "Studying Religion in Sub-Saharan Africa." In *Religion, Spirituality, and the Social Sciences: Challenging Marginalisation*, edited by B. Spalek and A. Imtoual, 79–91. Bristol, UK: Policy Press.

Frede, B., and J. Hill. 2014. "Introduction: Engendering Islamic Authority in West Africa." *Islamic Africa* 5 (2): 131–65.

Freedman, M. 1968. "Chinese Family Law in Singapore: The Rout of Custom." In *Family Law in Asia and Africa*, edited by J. N. D. Anderson, 49–72. London: Allen and Unwin.

Fukuyama, F. 1992. *The End of History and the Last Man*. New York: Free Press.

Gary, I. 2002. "Africa's Churches Wake Up to Oil's Problems and Possibilities." *Review of African Political Economy* 29 (91): 177–83.

Gbato, G. 2012. "Crise dans la coalition au pouvoir: Ouassénan koné à Ouattara; Nous sommes Libres. *Notre Voie*, no. 4271 (Nov. 17–18): 3–5.

Gifford, P. 1998. *African Christianity: Its Public Role*. London: Hurst.

———. 2015. *Christianity, Development, and Modernity in Africa*. London: Hurst.

Glodé, B. O. 2019. "Contexte politique de la modification du code de la famille en Côte d'Ivoire: Regards de la presse locale." In *Etat, Religions et Genre en Afrique Occidentale et Centrale*, edited by L. Lado and R. Yao Gnabeli, 53–72. Bamenda, Cameroon: Langaa RPCIG.

Gomez-Perez, M., ed. 2005. *L'islam politique au sud du Sahara: Identités, discours et enjeux*. Paris: Karthala.

Goodale, M. 2017. *Anthropology and Law: A Critical Introduction*. New York: New York University Press.

Gordon, D. F. 1992. "Conditionality in Policy-Based Lending in Africa. USAID experience." In *Development Finance and Policy Reform*, edited by P. Mosley, 394–411. London: Palgrave Macmillan.

Grubbs, L. 2009. *Secular Missionaries: Americans and African Development in the 1960s*. Amherst: University of Massachusetts Press.

Gueboguo, C. 2006. *La question homosexuelle en Afrique: Le cas du Cameroun*. Paris: L'Harmattan.

Hackett, R. I. J. 2000. "Power and Periphery: Studies of Gender and Religion in Africa." *Method and Theory in the Study of Religion* 12 (1): 238–44.

Hanson, J. 2014. "Religions in Africa." In *Africa*, 4th ed., edited by M. Grosz Ngaté and J. Hanson, 103–22. Bloomington: Indiana University Press.

Harshe, R. 2006. "Culture, Identity, and International Relations." *Economic and Political Weekly* 41 (37): 3945–51.

Hefner, R. 1998. "Multiple Modernities: Christianity, Islam, and Hinduism in a Globalizing Age." *Annual Review of Anthropology* 27:83–104.

Heinen, J. 2013. "Normes religieuses et statut des femmes par-delà nations etcontinents." In *Normes religieuses et genre: Mutations, résistances etreconfigurations, XIXe-XXIe Siècle*, edited by F. Rochefort and M. E. Sanna, 279–89. Paris: Armand Colin.

Hellsten, S. K. 2010. "Empowering the Invisible: Women, Local Culture, and Global Human Rights Protection." *Thought and Practice: A Journal of the Philosophical Association of Kenya (PAK)*, n.s., 2 (1): 37–57.

Hinfelaar, M. 2012. "Debating the Secular in Zambia: The Response of the Catholic Church to Scientific Socialism and Christian Nation, 1976–2006." In *Christianity and Public Culture in Africa*, edited by H. Englund, 50–66. Athens: Ohio University Press.

Hintzen, P. C. 2014. "After Modernization: Globalization and the African Dilemma." In *Modernization as Spectacle in Africa*, edited by P. J. Bloom, S. Miescher, and T. Manuh, 19–40. Bloomington: Indiana University Press.

Hodgson, D. 2017. *Gender, Justice, and the Problem of Culture: From Customary Law to Human Rights in Tanzania*. Bloomington: Indiana University Press.

Holder, G. 2013. "Un pays musulman en quête d'État-nation." In *La tragédie malienne*, edited by P. Gonin, N. Kotlok, and M. A. Pérouse de Montclos, 135–60. Paris: Editions Vendémiaire.

Hollenbach, D. 2002. *The Common Good and Christian Ethics*. Cambridge: Cambridge University Press.

Huttington, S. 1996. *Clashes of Civilizations and the Remaking of World Order*. New York: Simon and Schuster.

Ibhawoh, B. 2000. "Between Culture and Constitution: Evaluating the Cultural Legitimacy of Human Rights in the African State." *Human Rights Quarterly* 22 (3): 838–60.

Institut National de la Statistique de Côte d'Ivoire. 2009. Côte d'Ivoire - Etat Civil Abidjan (2006). http://www.ins.ci/n/nada/index.php/catalog/70/

sampling. Accessed Oct. 29, 2019.

———. 2014. *Recensement Général de la Population et de l'Habitat*, https:// www.ins.ci/documents/RGPH2014_expo_dg.pdf. Accessed September 9, 2022.

Institut National de la Statistique du Mali. 2015. *Consommation, pauvreté, bien-être des ménages, Avril 2014–Mars 2015.* http://mali.countrystat .org/fileadmin/user_upload/countrystat_fenix/congo/docs/ranuel14_eq .pdf. Accessed Oct. 29, 2019.

Itabohary, L. P. 2012. *Homophobie d'etat: Une enquête mondiale sur les lois qui criminalisent lasexualité entre adultes consentants du même sexe.* Brussels: ILGA.

Ivorian Government. 2009. *Document of National Policy on Equal Opportunities, Equity, and Gender.* Abidjan, Côte d'Ivoire.

Jeppie, S., E. Moosa, and R. Roberts. 2010a. Introduction to *Muslim Family Law in Sub-Saharan Africa: Colonial Legacies and Post-Colonial Challenges*, edited by S. Jeppie, E. Moosa, and R. Roberts, 13–60. Amsterdam: Amsterdam University Press.

———, eds. 2010b. *Muslim Family Law in Sub-Saharan Africa: Colonial Legacies and Post-Colonial Challenges.* Amsterdam: Amsterdam University Press.

Kane, H. 2008. *L'émergence d'un mouvement féministe au Sénégal. Le cas du Yewwu Yewwi.* Master's thesis, Département de sociologie, Faculté des lettres et sciences humaines, Université Cheikh Anta Diop, Dakar.

Kang, A. 2015. *Bargaining for Women's Rights: Activism in an Aspiring Muslim Democracy.* Minneapolis: University of Minnesota Press.

Kaplan, F. E., ed. 1997. *Queens, Queenmothers, Priestesses, and Power.* New York: New York Academy of Sciences.

Koffi, P. 2012. "Crise sur le projet de loi portant modification de la loi sur le mariage: Amadou Soumahoro sur RFI; Il y a parfois des incompréhensions qui doivent permettre au chefde famille, donc au président, de procéder à des réglages." *Le Nouveau Réveil*, no. 3240 (Nov. 17–18): 2–3.

Koné, M., and N. Kouame. 2005. *Socio-anthropologie de la famille en Afrique: Evolution desmodèles en Côte d'Ivoire.* Abidjan, Côte d'Ivoire: Les Editions du CERAP.

Kouakou, K. J. 2014. "Une famille sans chef est-elle réellement possible?" *European Scientific Journal* 10:207–15.

Kragbe, A. G. 2019. "L'évolution du code de la famille ivoirienne de 1964 à nos jours." In *Etat, Religions et Genre en Afrique Occidentale et Centrale*, edited by L. Lado and R. Yao Gnabeli, 73–102. Bamenda, Cameroon: Langaa RPCIG.

Kuenyehia, A. 1998. Introduction to *Women and Law in West Africa: Situational Analysis of Some Key Issues Affecting Women*, edited by K. Akua, ix–xvii. Accra: University of Ghana.

Kwok, P.-L. 2004. "Mercy Amba Oduyoye and African Women's Theology." *Journal of Feminist Studies in Religion* 20 (1): 7–22.

Kymlicka, W. 1995. *Multicultural Citizenship: A Liberal Theory of Minority Rights*. Oxford: Oxford University Press.

Lado, L. 2011. "L'homophobie populaire au Cameroun." *Cahier d'Etudes Africaines* 204. https://www.cairn-int.info/article-E_CEA_204_0921 --popular-homophobia-inCameroon.htm. Accessed Oct. 29, 2019.

———. 2012. "Le rôle public de l'Église Catholique en Afrique." *Études* 9 (417): 163–74.

Lamlili, N. 2003. "Sénégal: Une réforme à reculons du code de la famille." *L'Economiste*. http://www.leconomiste.com/article/senegal-une-reforme -reculons-du-code-de-la-famille. Accessed Oct. 29, 2019.

Lange, S., and M. Tjomsland. 2014. "Partnership, Policy Making, and Conditionality in the Gender Field: The Case of Tanzania. *Africa Today* 60 (4): 67–84.

Lasseur, M., and C. Mayrargue. 2011. "Le religieux dans la pluralisation contemporaine: Eclatement et concurrence." *Politique Africaine* 123:5–25.

LeBlanc, M. N. 2014. "Piety, Moral Agency, and Leadership: Dynamics around the Feminization of Islamic Authority in Côte d'Ivoire." *Islamic Africa* 5 (2): 167–98.

Lepape, M., and C. Vidal. 1984. "Libéralisme et vécus sexuels à Abidjan." *Cahiers Internationaux de Sociologie* 6:111–18.

Lévi-Strauss, C. 1969. *The Elementary Structures of Kinship*. Edited by R. Needham. Translated by J. H. Bell, J. R. von Sturmer, and R. Needham. Boston: Beacon.

Lutz, D. W. 2009. "African 'Ubuntu' Philosophy and Global Management. *Journal of Business Ethics* 84:313–28.

Macamo, E. 2005. "Introduction: Negotiating Modernity; From Colonialism to Globalization." In *Negotiating Modernity: Africa's Ambivalent Experience*, edited by E. Macamo, 1–16. Dakar, Senegal: Codesria Books.

Malinowski, B. 1943. "The Pan-African Problem of Culture Contact." *American Journal of Sociology* 48 (6): 649–65.

Malogne-Fer, G., and Y. Fer, eds. 2015. *Femmes et Pentecôtismes: Enjeux d'autorité et rapport de genre*. Geneva: Labor et Fides.

Manglos, N., and A. Weinreb. 2013. "Religion and Interest in Politics in Sub-Saharan Africa." *Social Forces* 92 (1): 195–219.

Maoulidi, S. 2017. "Between Law and Culture: Contemplating Rights for Women in Zanzibar." In *Gender and Culture at the Limit of Rights*, edited by D. Hodgson, 32–54. Philadelphia: University of Pennsylvania Press.

Marshall, C. 2017. "Gender Roles and Political, Social, and Economic Change in Bangladeshand, Senegal." In *Islam, Gender, and Democracy in Comparative Perspective*, edited by J. Cesari and J. Casanova, 139–59. New York: Oxford University Press.

Mayson, C. 2004. "A New Re-Formation: Religion, the State, and Gender." *Religion and Spirituality* 61:53–59.

Mbembe, A. 2017. *Critique of Black Reason*. Durham, NC: Duke University Press.

Mbow, P. 2010. "Contexte de la réforme du Code de la famille au Sénégal?" *Droit et cultures* 59:87–96.

Mercer, C. 2006. "Telecentres and Transformations: Modernizing Tanzania through the Internet." *African Affairs* 105 (419): 243–64.

Merry, S. E. 1992. "Anthropology, Law, and Transnational Processes." *Annual Review of Anthropology* 21:357–77.

———. 2006. "Transnational Human Rights and Local Activism: Mapping the Middle." *American Anthropologist* 108 (1): 38–51.

Mikell, G. 1995. "African Feminism: Toward a New Politics of Representation." *Feminist Studies* 21 (2): 405–24.

———, ed. 1997a. *African Feminism: The Politics of Survival in Sub-Saharan Africa*. Philadelphia: University of Pennsylvania Press.

———. 1997b. Introduction to *African Feminism: The Politics of Survival in Sub-Saharan Africa*, edited by G. Mikell, 1–50. Philadelphia: University of Pennsylvania Press.

Ministère de l'Intérieur et de la Sécurité de Côte d'Ivoire. 2017. *Annuaire Statistique D'Etat Civil 2017*. http://www.infomie.net/IMG/pdf/annu aire_statistique_etat_civ_2017.pdf. Accessed Oct. 29, 2019.

Miran-Guyon, M. 2006. "The Political Economy of Civil Islam in Côte d'Ivoire." In *PolitischerIslam in West-Afrika: Eine Bestandsaufnahme*, edited by M. Bröningand and H. Weiss, 82–113. Berlin: Friedrich Ebert Stiftung-Lit Verlag.

Moore, S. F. 1969. "Law and Anthropology." *Biennial Review of Anthropology* 6:252–300.

Morton, A. 2007. *Unravelling Gramsci: Hegemony and Passive Revolution in the Global Political Economy*. London: Pluto.

Msibi, T. 2011. "The Lies We Have Been Told: On (Homo) Sexuality in Africa." *Africa Today* 58 (1): 55–77.

Murithi, T. 2009. "An African Perspective on Peace Education: Ubuntu Lessons in Reconciliation." *International Review of Education* 55 (2/3): 221–33.

Murray, S. O., and W. Roscoe, eds. 1998. *Boy-Wives and Female Husbands: Studies in African Homosexualities.* New York: St. Martin's.

Nabudere, D. W. 1997. "Beyond Modernization and Development, or, Why the Poor Reject Development." *Geografiska Annaler: Series B, Human Geography* 79 (4): 203–15.

National Institute of Statistics. 2014. *Rapport du recensement général de la population et de l'habitat de Côte d'Ivoire.* http://www.ins.ci/n/documents/RGPH2014_expo_dg.pdf. Accessed Oct. 29, 2019.

N'Diaye, M. 2016. *La réforme du droit de la famille: Une comparaison Sénégal-Maroc.* http://books.openedition.org/pum/3364. Accessed Oct. 29, 2019.

Njambi, W. N., and W. E. O'Brien. 2005. "Revisiting 'Woman-Woman Marriage': Notes on Gikuyu Women." In *African Studies of Gender: A Reader*, edited by O. Oyewumi, 143–65. New York: Palgrave Macmillan.

Njoh, A., and F. Akiwumi. 2012. "The Impact of Religion on Women's Empowerment as a Millennium Development Goal in Africa." *Social Indicators Research* 107 (1): 1–18.

Nnaemeka, O. 2005. "Mapping African Feminisms." In *Readings in Gender in Africa*, edited by A. Cornwall, 31–41. London: International African Institute.

Nozick, R. 1974. *Anarchy, State, and Utopia.* New York: Basic Books.

Oakley, A. 1972. *Sex, Gender, and Society.* London: Temple Smith.

Otayek, R. 1993. "De nouveaux intellectuels musulmans d'Afrique noire." In *Le radicalisme islamique au Sud du Sahara*, edited by R. Otayek, 7–18. Paris: Karthala.

Ouattara, L. 2012a. "Projet de loi sur le mariage en Côte d'Ivoire: La loi votée hier à la quasi-unanimité." *Le Patriote*, no. 3901 (Nov. 22): 4–6.

———. 2012b. "Soro Guillaume: La bonne loi, c'est celle qui traverse les siècles." *Le Patriote*, no. 3901 (Nov. 22): 2–4.

———. 2012c. "Yasmina Ouégnin opposée à la promotion de la femme." *Le Patriote*, no. 3901 (Nov. 22): 14–16.

Oyewumi, O., ed. 2005a. *African Gender Studies: A Reader.* New York: Palgrave Macmillan.

———. 2005b. "Visualizing the Body: Western Theories and African Subjects." In *African Studies of Gender: A Reader*, edited by O. Oyewumi, 3–21. New York: Palgrave Macmillan.

Oyono-Mbia, G. 1964. *Trois prétendants . . . un mari.* Yaoundé: Editions CLE.

Parsitau, D. 2012. "Arise, Oh Ye Daughters of Faith: Women, Pentecostalism, and Public Culture in Kenya." In *Christianity and Public Culture in Africa*, edited by H. England, 131–49. Athens: Ohio University Press.

Pellerin, M., and Y. Trotignon. 2010. "Les enjeux sécuritaires du rivage sahélien." *Sécurité et stratégie* 4 (2): 43–56.

Pereira, C., and J. Ibrahim. 2010. "On the Bodies of Women: The Common Ground between Islam and Christianity in Nigeria." *Third World Quarterly* 31 (6): 921–37.

Perrot, C.-H. 2005. "Du visible à l'invisible: Les supports du pouvoir en pays akan (Afrique del'ouest)." *Bulletin du Centre de recherche du château de Versailles*. DOI: 10.4000/crcv.359.

Pew Research Center. 2010. *Tolerance and Tension: Islam and Christianity in Sub-Saharan Africa.* https://www.pewforum.org/2010/04/15/executive-summary-islam-and-christianity-in-sub-saharan-africa/. Accessed Oct. 29, 2019.

———. 2015. *The Future of World Religions: Population Growth Projections, 2010–2050.* http://www.globalreligiousfutures.org/countries/senegal#/?affiliations_religion_id=0&affliations_year=2020&region_name=All%20Countries&restrictions_year=2015. Accessed Oct. 29, 2019.

Pickbourn, L., and L. Ndikumana. 2016. "The Impact of the Sectoral Allocation of Foreign Aid on Gender Inequality." *Journal of International Development* 28 (3): 396–411.

Portier, P. 2005. "L'Église catholique face au modèle français de laïcité: Histoire d'un Ralliement." *Archives de sciences sociales des religions* 129 (50): 117–34.

———. 2013. "La construction religieuse du genre: Remarques sur un processus ambivalent." In *Normes religieuses et genre: Mutations, résistances et reconfiguration (XIXᵉ-XXIᵉ siècle)*, edited by F. Rochefort, 303–10. Paris: Armand Colin.

Portier, P., and I. Théry. 2015. "Du mariage civil au 'mariage pour tous': Sécularisation du droit et mobilisations catholiques." *Sociologie* 6 (1): 81–104.

Radcliffe-Brown, A. R., and Forde, Daryll, eds. 1950. *African Systems of Kinship and Marriage.* London: Oxford University Press.

Rathbone, R. 2002. "West Africa: Modernity and Modernization." In *African Modernities*, edited by J.-G. Deutsch, P. Probst, and H. Schmidt, 18–30. Portsmouth, NH: Heinemann.

Rawls, J. 1971. *A Theory of Justice*. Oxford: Oxford University Press.

———. 1993. *Political Liberalism*. New York: Columbia University Press.

Razavi, S., and A. Jenichen. 2010. "The Unhappy Marriage of Religion and Politics: Problems and Pitfalls for Gender Equality." *Third World Quarterly* 31 (6): 833–50.

Rivière, C. 1997. "Religion et politique en Afrique." *Anthropos* 92 (1–2): 21–34.

Rochefort, F., and M. E. Sanna. 2013. Introduction to *Normes religieuses et genre: Mutations, résistances et reconfigurations, XIXe-XXIe Siècle*, edited by F. Rochefort and M. E. Sanna, 11–21. Paris: Armand Colin.

Rohrs, S., and D. Smythe. 2014. Introduction to *In search of Equality: Women, Law, and Society in Africa*, edited by S. Rohrs, A. Hsieh, and M. de Souza, 1–18. Cape Town: University of Cape Town Press.

Ruggie, J. 1983. "Human Rights and the Future International Community." *Daedalus* 112 (4): 93–110.

Sackey, B. M. 2006. *New Directions in Gender and Religion*. Lanham, MD: Lexington.

Sadie, Y. 2002. "Aid and Political Conditionalities in Sub-Saharan Africa." *South African Journal of International Affairs* 9 (1): 57–68.

Samaké, B. 2019. "Un Retour sur l'Expérience Avortée de la Révision du Code des Personnes et de la Famille au Mali." *Etat, Religions, et Genre en Afrique Occidentale et Centrale*, edited by L. Lado and R. Yao Gnabeli, 123–37. Bamenda, Cameroon: Langaa RPCIG.

Sandel, M. 1982. *Liberalism and the Limits of Justice*. Cambridge: Cambridge University Press.

———. 1984. "The Procedural Republic and the Unencumbered Self." *Political Theory* 12:81–96.

Sangare, Y., and T. Lath. 2012. "La femme n'est pas chef de la famille, la loi ne le dit pas." *Le Patriote*, no. 3900 (Nov. 21): 4–7.

Sarr, F. 2019. "Du code de la famille de 1972 à la loi sur la parité de 2010 au Sénégal." In *Etat, Religions, et Genre en Afrique Occidentale et Centrale*, edited by L. Lado and R. Yao Gnabeli, 105–25. Bamenda, Cameroon: Langaa RPCIG.

Saw, M. 2017. "Figures of the Week: Employment and Labor Productivity in Côte d'Ivoire." (Aug. 23) Brookings Institution. https://www.brookings .edu/blog/africa-in-focus/2017/08/23/figures-of-the-week-employment-and-labor-productivity-in-cote-divoire/. Accessed Oct. 29, 2019.

Schröter, S. 2017. "Islamic Feminism: National and Transnational Dimensions." In *Islam, Gender, and Democracy in Comparative Perspective*, edited by J. Cesari and J. Casanova, 113–36. New York: Oxford University Press.

Schulz, D. E. 2003. "Political Factions, Ideological Fictions: The Controversy over Family Law Reform in Democratic Mali." *Islamic Law and Society* 10 (1): 132–64.

Semien, E. A. 2012. "Dissolution du gouvernement: L'APDH condamne la décision." *Notre Voie*, no. 4271 (Nov. 17–18): 3–4.

Sklar, R. L. 1995. "The New Modernization." *Issue: A Journal of Opinion* 23 (1): 19–21.

Smith, J. H. 2012. "Religious Dimensions of Conflict and Peace in Neoliberal Africa: An Introduction." In *Displacing the State: Religion and Conflict in Neoliberal Africa*, edited by J. H. Smith and R. I. J. Hackett, 1–23. Notre Dame, IN: University of Notre Dame Press.

Soares, B. F. 2005. "Islam in Mali in the Neoliberal Era." *African Affairs* 105 (418): 77–95.

———. 2009. "The Attempt to Reform Family Law in Mali." *Die Welt des Islams* 49 (3/4): 398–428.

Sounaye, A. 2009. "Ambiguous Secularism: Islam, Laïcité, and the State in Niger." *Civilisations* 58 (2): 41–57.

Ssenyonjo, M. 2007. "Culture and the Human Rights of Women in Africa: Between Light and Shadow." *Journal of African Law* 51 (1): 39–67.

Starr, J., and J. Collier, eds. 1989. *History and Power in the Study of Law: New Directions in Legal Anthropology*. Ithaca, NY: Cornell University Press.

Stoeckl, K. 2014. *The Russian Orthodox Church and Human Rights*. London: Routledge.

Takoue, S. 2012. "Crise sur le projet de loi portant modification de la loi sur le mariage: Babacar Justin N'Diaye; Ouattara fait l'affaire des pro-Gbagbo." *Le Nouveau Réveil*, no. 3240 (Nov. 17–18): 3–4.

Taylor, C. 1992. *The Malaise of Modernity*. Concord, Canada: Anansi.

Tesfai, Y. 2010. *Holy Warriors, Infidels, and Peacemakers in Africa*. New York: Palgrave Macmillan.

Tim, M. 2012. "Projet de loi sur le mariage: Les députés ont voté avec 213 voix sur 229." *Le Jour Plus*, no. 2595 (Nov. 22): 3–4.

Toungara, J. M. 1994. "Inventing the African family: Gender and Family Law Reform in Côte d'Ivoire." *Journal of Social History* 28 (1): 37–61.

Touré, A. 1981. *La civilisation quotidienne en Côte d'Ivoire. Procès d'occidentalisation.* Paris: Karthala.

Traoré, A. 2012. "Amendement de la loi de 1964 relative au mariage: Imam Dosso Mamadou, secrétaire général du conseil national islamique." *Le Jour Plus*, no. 2593 (Nov. 20): 6–7.

Trinitapoli, J. 2006. "Religious responses to AIDS in Sub-Saharan Africa: An Examination of Religious Congregations in Rural Malawi." *Review of Religious Research* 47 (3): 253–70.

Unesco Institute for Statistics. 2017. Country profile of Côte d'Ivoire. http://uis.unesco.org/fr/country/ci. Accessed Oct. 29, 2019.

United Nations Development Programme. 2020. Gender Inequality Index (GII). https://hdr.undp.org/data-center/specific-country-data#/countries/CIV. Accessed August 20, 2022.

Vangroenweghe, D. 2000. *Sida et sexualité en Afrique.* Brussels: Editions EPO.

Van Hoyweghen, S. 1996. "The Disintegration of the Catholic Church of Rwanda: A Study of the Fragmentation of Political and Religious Authority." *African Affairs* 95 (380): 379–401.

Vimard, P. 1993. "Modernité et pluralité familiales en Afrique de l'Ouest." *Tiers-Monde* 34 (133): 89–115. https://doi.org/10.3406/tiers.1993.4828. Accessed Oct. 29, 2019.

Vléï-Yoroba, C. 1997. "Droit de la famille et réalités familiales: Le cas de la Côte d'Ivoire depuis l'indépendance. *Clio: Histoire, femmes et sociétés* 6. http://clio.revues.org/383. Accessed Oct. 29, 2019.

Woodhead, L. 2013. "Gender Differences in Religious Practice and Significance." *International Scientific Researchers* 13:58–85.

World Economic Forum. 2017. *The Global Gender Gap Report Index, 2017.* http://www3.weforum.org/docs/WEF_GGGR_2017.pdf. Accessed Oct. 29, 2019.

Yao, K. E., et al. 2012. "Description du vécu des homosexuels masculins suivis dans une clinique de la ville d'Abidjan (Côte d'Ivoire)." *Psy Cause* 61:17–25.

INDEX

Abidjan
  civil marriage survey, 37–56
  marriage law reform survey,
    57–93
African Development Bank, 105
African traditional religions, 59
arranged marriage, 1–2, 46

Bédié, Henri Konan, 24
Bela, E., 34
bride price. *See* bride wealth
bride wealth
  Cameroon, 1–2
  in customary marriage, 42–43
  and the family code (Côte
    d'Ivoire), 39
  and husband's authority, 43
  and legitimacy of paternity, 43
  male ownership of wife and
    children, 11
  prohibition, 39, 51, 118

Cameroon, 1–3
Catholicism
  gender issues, 61
  and marriage, 47
  men's views of modernity, 81–82
  and 2013 marriage law, 67–71

women's views of modernity, 66,
  68–69
See also religion
CEDAW. *See* Convention on the
  Elimination of All Forms of
  Discrimination against Women
children
  authority over, 38
  legal paternity (legitimacy), 44,
    99
  of previous unions, 51
Christianity
  introduction to Africa, 62–63
  and marriage, 47
  See also religion
civil marriage, 37, 43
  age difference between spouses,
    46
  benefits for women, 44
  characteristics of spouses, 45–54
  choice of residence, 55
  cost, 55
  education of spouses, 48
  employment of spouses, 52–53
  ethnicity, 48
  and management of property, 54
  nationality, 48
  prevalence, 43, 45

LUDOVIC LADO

Ludovic Lado holds a doctorate in social anthropology
from Oxford University and is director of the
Jesuit Center for Studies and Training for Development
(CEFOD) in N'Djamena, Chad. He is the author of
Catholic Pentecostalism and the Paradoxes of Africanization.